PROVINCIAL FACILITATION FOR INVESTMENT AND TRADE INDEX

GENDER ANALYSIS FOR MEASURING ECONOMIC GOVERNANCE FOR BUSINESS DEVELOPMENT IN THE LAO PEOPLE'S DEMOCRATIC REPUBLIC

SECOND EDITION

MARCH 2022

Creative Commons Attribution 3.0 IGO license (CC BY 3.0 IGO)

Notes:
In this publication, "$" refers to United States dollars and "KN" refers to Lao kip.
ADB recognizes "Laos" as the Lao People's Democratic Republic and "Vietnam" as Viet Nam.

On the cover: Improving the quality of economic governance for both women and men is essential for driving a more dynamic business environment in the Lao People's Democratic Republic. The data captured in the Provincial Facilitation for Investment and Trade (ProFIT) survey provide important insights on the experiences of the private sector in conducting their business activities throughout the country.

Cover design by Mike Cortes.

Contents

Tables, Figures, and Box   v

Foreword   vii

Acknowledgments   ix

Author Profiles   xi

Abbreviations   xii

Executive Summary   xiii

1   Introduction   1

2   Women's Participation in Business: A Contextual Background   3

     A. Laws and Institutions for Gender Equality   4

     B. Key Constraints to Women's Effective Participation   6

     C. The Shape of Women's Enterprises   10

     D. Comparative Economic Governance Surveys and Gender   13

3   ProFIT Survey   15

     A. Methodology and Respondent Profiles   16

         1. Methodology   16

         2. Scoring Methodology   17

         3. Respondent Profiles   18

     B. Result of ProFIT 2019 from a Gender Perspective   20

         1. Scores of Women and Men in Enterprises   20

         2. Starting a Business   20

         3. Transparency and Access to Information   22

         4. Regulatory Burden   24

         5. Informal Charges   25

         6. Consistency in Policy Implementation   28

         7. Business Friendliness   29

4   Selected Issues   31

     A. Facilitating the Transition from the Informal to the Formal Economy   32

     B. Impact of PMO 02/2018 on Women in Enterprises   33

     C. Collating Further Gender-Disaggregated Data for Assessment   33

Contents

5   Conclusions and Policy Implications   35

Appendix 1   40

Appendix 2   41

References   49

Tables, Figures, and Box

Tables

1	Summary of Gender Equality Laws	4
2	Location of Household Head's Business	7
3	Enterprises with Access to Finance	8
4	Usage of ICT Tools in a Business	9
5	Business Registration	10
6	Reasons for Not Registering a Business	11
7	Type of Social Pension Scheme	11
8	Three Main Sectors of Activity	12
9	Methodology for Computing the 2019 ProFIT Index	17
10	Examples of Licenses Required for Different Business Activities	22

Figures

1	Enterprises' Leadership by Gender	10
2	ProFIT Index Components	16
3	Enterprises' Ownership, Leadership, and Both by Sex	18
4	Women-Led and Men-Led Enterprises by Sector	19
5	Women-Led and Men-Led Enterprises by Size	19
6	ProFIT Score for Ownership and Leadership by Gender	20
7	Starting a Business for Ownership and Leadership by Gender	21
8	Cost of Business Registration for Ownership and Leadership by Gender	21
9	Transparency and Access to Information Subindex for Leadership and Ownership by Gender	23
10	Transparency and Access to Information Subindex by Gender and Enterprise Size	23
11	Access to Three Key Official Documents	24
12	Cost and Time for Renewing Tax Identification Number	25
13	Informal Charges Subindex for Leadership and Ownership by Gender	26
14	Selected Indicators of Informal Charges for Leadership and Ownership by Gender	26
15	Consistency of Policy Implementation Subindex for Leadership and Ownership by Gender	28
16	Selected Indicators of Consistency in Policy Implementation for Leadership and Ownership by Gender	28

17   Business Friendliness Subindex for Leadership and Ownership by Gender   29
18   Knowledge of PMO 02/2018 for Leadership and Ownership by Gender   30
19   Time and Cost to Obtain an Enterprise Registration Certificate   34
      with Knowledge of PMO 02/2018 by Gender

Box

Informal Practices in Business Operations in the Lao People's Democratic Republic   27

Foreword

The Lao National Chamber of Commerce and Industry (LNCCI) is proud to launch the *Provincial Facilitation for Investment and Trade Index (ProFIT)–Gender Analysis for Measuring Economic Governance for Business Development* report for the Lao People's Democratic Republic (Lao PDR). The LNCCI would also like to express sincere thanks to the Asian Development Bank for its support during the survey preparation and consultation process with relevant government agencies and development partners in the country.

This report, the first of its kind, sheds light on women's participation in economic activities and the constraints that women entrepreneurs face in doing business in the Lao PDR. It draws on data obtained from a survey of 1,357 enterprises on key business indicators, as well as data from the Lao Statistics Bureau and key informant interviews, to provide a nuanced analysis of the experiences of women and men in the workplace.

The report documents progress made by the government in improving the regulatory environment for businesses and in promoting gender equality. It also raises awareness on the importance of accelerating reforms to improve the business environment for a more inclusive growth in the Lao PDR. In particular, the report sheds light on issues related to transparency and access to information that impact upon business opportunities that are available to women entrepreneurs. Solutions to this challenge are at hand, with the government taking proactive measures to improve regulatory compliance by consolidating requirements and shifting many of its services online.

The key findings and policy recommendations of this report provide a basis for the LNCCI to engage in dialogue with the government for improving the implementation of policy and regulations to support women entrepreneurs. The LNCCI is committed to continuing to work with both government agencies and development partners to promote gender equality and more women entrepreneurs in the Lao PDR. Our goal is to provide greater access to business opportunities for both women and men for moving toward a more inclusive growth model for all across the country.

Oudet Souvannavong
President
Lao National Chamber of Commerce and Industry

Foreword

The *Gender Analysis for Measuring Economic Governance for Business Development* report was prepared in parallel with the second report on the Provincial Facilitation for Investment and Trade Index (ProFIT) for the Lao People's Democratic Republic (Lao PDR). These reports combined provide a nuanced analysis of the experiences of women and men in doing business in the country. A recurrent theme that emerges in both reports is on the issue of transparency and access to information. With access to information an issue, the report finds that businesswomen have benefited comparably less from business environment reforms introduced to date.

To improve equity in the business environment, it will be important that further consideration is given to the gender dimensions of regulation and the services that support its implementation. Key initiatives, including raising awareness to improve regulatory compliance, leveraging the benefits of technology for improving access to information, and developing gender-inclusive policies, will help to drive a speedy and more inclusive pandemic recovery.

The Asian Development Bank is proud to have partnered with the Lao National Chamber of Commerce and Industry in preparing this report. We are equally grateful to the Ministry of Commerce and Industry for its strategic guidance and support throughout the duration of the study. Review by development partners, including the World Bank and the International Monetary Fund, helped with strengthen the report and highlights the priority given to gender equity on the national, regional, and international agendas.

I believe this report will serve as a valuable reference for informing dialogue toward a more inclusive regulatory environment for business that benefits both women and men. Combined with the recently published *Measuring Economic Governance for Business Development in the Lao PDR* report, the challenges in the business environment and options to address them are well understood. If implemented, the ideas contained herein will contribute to improved enterprise sustainability and provide strong foundations for a vibrant private sector-led post-pandemic recovery.

Ramesh Subramaniam
Director General
Southeast Asia Department
Asian Development Bank

Acknowledgments

The *Provincial Facilitation for Investment and Trade Index (ProFIT) Gender Analysis for Measuring Economic Governance for Business Development* was prepared by the Asian Development Bank (ADB) under a regional technical assistance project (RETA 9387), Strengthening Institutions for Localizing Agenda 2030 for Sustainable Development, which was generously supported by the Poverty Reduction and Regional Cooperation Fund of the Government of the People's Republic of China. This study was undertaken by the Lao People's Democratic Republic (Lao PDR) Resident Mission (LRM) of ADB. LRM Country Director Sonomi Tanaka provided strategic guidance on the study. The study was completed under the supervision of Senior Country Economist Emma Allen of the LRM. Phantouleth Louangraj of the LRM and Mai Lin Villaruel of the Macroeconomic Research Division of Economic Research and Regional Cooperation Department provided valuable technical support for the study. Maylee Phommachanh of the LRM provided administrative support. Souphavanh Phonmany of the LRM provided support for printing and publication request. Theonakhet Saphakdy of the LRM provided technical advice on gender-related matters. Vijaya Nagarajan, independent gender consultant, provided technical leadership in preparing the study. Phan Vinh Quang, independent consultant, and Bounlert Vanhnalat of the National University of the Lao PDR, led the survey of enterprises, including the design of the survey methodology and supervision of the data collection, data analysis, and sharing of preliminary findings with key stakeholders. The data collection team of the Lao National Chamber of Commerce and Industry (LNCCI) consisted of Phouxay Thepphavong, Phonevilay Sinavong, Souphaphone Khamsennam, Daovading Phirasayphithak, Phutthasone Phomvisay, Manitto Phomphothi, Phongsavanh Phetvorlasak, Keomanivone Sayavongsa, Pkoumy Phommivong, Jenjila Chanthasom, Nongthong Vongsavanh, Souphanthong Phonseya, Khamsone Chanthasili, Khonesavanh Chathavong, Lathtekone Sengdeuanphet, and Souksavanh Atsanavong.

Under the guidance of Hanif Rahemtulla and Rachana Shrestha, Marjorie Anne Javillonar, Abigail Armamento, and Rainer Maria Rene Rohdewohld of the Governance Thematic Group at ADB provided support for technical assistance and implementation. This study benefited from invaluable comments received from peer reviewers including Dominic Patrick Mellor of the Office of the Director General of the Private Sector Operations Department; Robert Lockhart, Vissia Camille Guarico, and Jackie Surtani of Infrastructure Finance Division 2 of the Private Sector Operations Department; Amanda Satterly and Neeti Katoch of the Private Sector Transportation Support Division of the Private Sector Operations Department; Daisuke Mizusawa, Hiroaki Yamaguchi, and Gengwen Zhao of the Transport and Communications Division, of the Southeast Asia Department; Mendizabal Joffre and Veronica Mendizabal Joffre of the Office of the Director General of the Southeast Asia Department; Srinivas Sampath, Steven Schipani, and Judie Ann Militar of the Urban Development and Water Division of the Southeast Asia Department; Elaine Thomas of the Office of the Cluster Head of the Sustainable Development and Climate Change Department; Aiko Kikkawa Takenaka and Lei Lei Song of the Economic Analysis and Operational Support Division of the Economic Research and Regional Cooperation Department; and Keiko Nowacka and Samantha Hung of the Gender Equality Thematic Group of the Sustainable Development and Climate Change Department. ADB's Department of Communications provided a final review and support in printing and web publication of the report.

This study is a product of extensive consultations with key government ministries in the Lao PDR and their agencies. We are especially grateful to Lattanaphone Vongsuthi, Sengxay Phousinghao, and Simmavanh Vayouphack of Ministry of Industry and Commerce, whose insights have been instrumental to the study.

We are grateful to the advisers including Oudet Souvannavong, Valy Vetsaphong, Xaybandith Rasphone, Bounleuth Luangpaseuth, and Vanthong Sithikoun of the LNCCI for guidance provided throughout the study.

Last, we would like to extend our thanks to external stakeholders and development partners for their generosity in supporting the peer review of this publication, with supportive comments and strategic guidance helping to improve the quality of analysis and recommendations substantially. In particular, thanks go to Dan Heldon, Hannah Wurf, and Soulivanh Souksavath of the Government of Australia; Painchaud Francois and Anousa Khounnavong of the International Monetary Fund; Todd Wassel, Tamara Failor, and Sisavan Phimmasan of the Asia Foundation; and Melise Jaud, Alexander Kremer, and Aiden Be Benedict Glendinning of the World Bank Group.

Author Profiles

Emma Allen is a senior country economist at the Lao People's Democratic Republic Resident Mission (LRM) of the Asian Development Bank (ADB). Her current responsibilities include heading the economics, strategy, and programming unit of the LRM. She prepares the Lao People's Democratic Republic (Lao PDR) chapter for ADB's flagship publication, *Asian Development Outlook,* as well as ADB's country programming and strategy documents for the Lao PDR. She also supports the design and implementation of ADB loans and technical assistance related to public financial management, reform of state-owned enterprises, United Nations (UN) Sustainable Development Goals, knowledge and analytical support, and business environment. Prior to joining ADB in 2016, she was a labor market economist with the International Labour Organization. She received her doctor of philosophy (PhD) degree in economics and her bachelor's degree in combined economics and education from the University of Newcastle, Australia, in 2015 and 2004, respectively.

Phantouleth Louangraj is a senior economics officer at the LRM of ADB. He is responsible for private sector operations, technical assistance, and knowledge under the economics, strategy, and programming unit of the LRM. He administers projects and technical assistance to support private sector development. Prior to ADB, he joined the UN Development Programme (UNDP) as a project officer. He obtained his master's degree in business administration from Waseda University, Japan, in 2004.

Mai Lin Villaruel is an economics officer in the Macroeconomics Research Division of the Economic Research and Regional Cooperation Department of ADB. She is part of the team that produces *Asian Development Outlook* and *Asia Bond Monitor.* She holds a master's degree in applied statistics from Macquarie University in Sydney, Australia.

Vijaya Nagarajan is a consultant working on the intersection of development, gender, and economic regulation. Her areas of expertise are economic empowerment of women, inclusive policy and law reform, and private sector development. Vijaya is an emeritus professor at Macquarie University in Sydney and has researched and published widely on these areas.

Phan Vinh Quang is a development consultant and has worked on a number of assignments for ADB, the United States Agency for International Development, the International Finance Corporation, UNDP, and Australia's Department of Foreign Affairs and Trade, among others. He helped with the partnership between the Vietnam Chamber of Commerce and Industry and the Lao National Chamber of Commerce and Industry on the development of Provincial Facilitation for Investment and Trade (ProFIT) in 2017 and 2019. He has worked with both the public and private sectors on commercializing technologies, promoting entrepreneurship, value chain development, regulatory reforms, and trade liberalization. He runs a small consulting firm serving international clients in Viet Nam. He has a master's degree in business administration from the University of Bath, United Kingdom, and a bachelor's degree from the Foreign Trade University, Viet Nam.

Bounlert Vanhnalat is a junior economist at the National University of the Lao PDR, Faculty of Economic and Business Management. He has a research background in international trade and enterprises development in the Lao PDR. He worked as the national consultant for an assessment of ProFIT in the Lao PDR in 2018, and worked with the Ministry of Industry and Commerce to assess the impact of the Association of Southeast Asian Nations (ASEAN) Economic Community on the Lao PDR's economy under the regional economic integration of the Lao PDR into ASEAN and entrepreneurship development. He obtained a PhD in economics from Kobe University, Japan in 2012.

Abbreviations

ADB	–	Asian Development Bank
ASEAN	–	Association of Southeast Asian Nations
CEO	–	chief executive officer
COVID-19	–	coronavirus disease
ICT	–	information and communication technology
LRM	–	Lao People's Democratic Republic Resident Mission
Lao PDR	–	Lao People's Democratic Republic
LNCCI	–	Lao National Chamber of Commerce and Industry
ProFIT	–	Provincial Facilitation for Investment and Trade
PMO	–	Prime Minister's Order
SDG	–	Sustainable Development Goal
TIN	–	tax identification number

Executive Summary

The *Provincial Facilitation for Investment and Trade Index (ProFIT) Gender Analysis for Measuring Economic Governance for Business Development* report analyzes women and men's experiences of doing business in the Lao People's Democratic Republic (Lao PDR) at local government levels. It demonstrates how women and men are impacted differently by the same regulations and illustrates the hidden bias inherent in a "one-size-fits-all" approach. It makes key recommendations to address this bias and calls for greater collaboration in developing gender-responsive approaches.

In 2018, the Government of the Lao PDR adopted Prime Minister's Order No. 02 (PMO 02/2018), which aims to improve the country's business environment by simplifying the process for obtaining business registration. It does so by allowing for tax identification numbers (TINs) and business registration certificates to be obtained at the same time. The ProFIT survey data and related reports share information on the responses of 1,357 enterprises in 17 provinces and seek to measure the impact of PMO 02/2018. This report shares findings from the second round of data collection that was completed at the end of 2019 and builds on the first survey from 2017. The 2019 survey incorporated a range of questions aimed at gathering gender-disaggregated data.

This report brings together the ProFIT survey data with supplementary data from the Lao Statistics Bureau to conduct a gender analysis of enterprises in the Lao PDR. It focuses on six key areas: (i) ease of starting a business, (ii) transparency and access to information, (iii) regulatory burden, (iv) informal charges, (v) consistency in policy implementation, and (vi) business friendliness of the provincial administrations.

Key finding 1: Women-led enterprises had lower levels of compliance and tended to be smaller in size than men-led enterprises.

Nearly 70% of the Lao PDR's 133,000 businesses operate informally and women are more likely than men to do so. This represents noncompliance as all business activities, unless exempt, must comply with existing regulations on business registration, licensing rules, and tax laws. One in four women had a registration certificate compared with one in three men. Women are less likely to get a business license, a tax registration certificate, or participate in social security schemes than their male counterparts. Only 10.9% of women-led enterprises reported having a TIN compared to 15.5% of men-led enterprises.

Part of the reason for noncompliance is because women-led enterprises were overrepresented in microenterprise categories, with 45.1% of women-led enterprises being microenterprises compared to 30.8% of men-led enterprises. Such enterprises have fewer workers, lower profits, and less awareness of laws and regulations. Further, only 35% of women-led enterprises had plans for expansion, compared to 65% of men-led enterprises, which has implications for policy development.

Key finding 2: Women-led enterprises incur greater time and costs than men-led enterprises during registration relative to enterprise size.

At first glance, the 2019 survey indicates that women took less time to register a business, with 27% of women-led businesses reporting the process was completed in fewer than 10 days, while the average women-led enterprise took 28 days for registration. This is a considerable improvement from 2017 when it took 50 days to complete this process. However, taking into account the type and size of women-run enterprises, a different picture emerges. Women-owned and -led enterprises are predominantly microenterprises engaged in the provision of services and trade such as small retail stores, which require fewer licenses and permits. For example, opening a retail store, predominately women-owned, requires two licenses compared to a manufacturing business, predominately men-owned that requires up to 13 licenses, which would be reflected in the time taken and cost paid for starting the business.

Similarly, the 2019 survey indicates that starting a business was less costly for women-led enterprises. It shows that women-led enterprises paid on average KN2.1 million for business registration compared to KN2.7 million paid by men-led enterprises. However, when compared to the size of the enterprise, women-owned and led firms paid one-third more than their male counterparts.

Key finding 3: Lack of transparency erodes trust in government, with implications for access to business opportunities for businesswomen.

Women-led enterprises identified transparency and access to official documents at the provincial level to be significant issues that they face in doing business. Analysis of data collected through ProFIT indicates that women gave lower scores on the subindexes of transparency and access to information than men-led enterprises when it came to obtaining information from provincial governments. Only 29.5% of women-led enterprises reported that they had access to necessary procedures and forms compared to 34.6% of men-led enterprises. They were also critical of the ability of provincial governments to apply national laws. They stated that poor access to information led to a perceived need to pay informal charges to ensure smooth business operations. More women-led and women-owned enterprises, compared to their male counterparts, expressed a lack of trust in provincial governments, stating that enterprises benefited economically from such personal connections with government officials.

Key finding 4: Informal charges add additional burden on businesswomen.

Informal charges are non-official payments made to access registration processes, obtain licenses, and determine how much tax is to be paid. While such payments are clearly prohibited, the ProFIT survey found that 70% of respondents made such payments. While both women-led and women-owned enterprises as well as men-led and men-owned enterprises recognized that such payments were necessary, some of these charges weighed more heavily on women. While 71.6% of women-owned enterprises reported that tax negotiations were common, 67.9% of men-owned enterprises reported the same. Such charges place a heavy burden on micro and small businesses where women dominate. It means that many choose to operate informally, avoiding the formal and informal costs of registration, thereby hindering the growth of a competitive private sector and an effective tax base for the government.

Key finding 5: Women entrepreneurs had less access to knowledge and technical skills.

Only 29% of women-led enterprises were aware of PMO 02/2018, which aims to facilitate businesses' entry into the market, compared with 71% of men-led enterprises. This is most likely due to women's poor networks, compared to men's networks, that help publicize regulatory changes. Such lack of awareness is also indicative of other deficits such as skills in online marketing, use of information and communication technology (ICT), and technology solutions for business activities. It is reported that only 2.2% of women-led enterprises used ICT to sell their products while 3.3% of men-led enterprises did the same, attesting to the need for greater attention to skills development. Furthermore, only 35.9% of women-led enterprises used accounting programs in their business while 64.1% of men-led enterprises did so, making compliance more onerous and negotiations of tax liability more discretionary.

Policy Recommendations

Improving the implementation of PMO 02/2018 in accordance with aims will involve diverse stakeholders, including government departments, business associations, businesses, and civil society. A detailed list of 16 recommendations is discussed in this report, of which the key initiatives include addressing regulatory change and implementation, improving access to information, developing gender-inclusive policies, and raising awareness on compliance.

Government departments should take the lead on improving regulatory compliance through two main initiatives: (i) The Ministry of Industry and Commerce has started work on the electronic registration system and an inventory of licenses. It should ensure that its awareness campaigns reach women and it should introduce help desks to assist women entrepreneurs and provide training to their staff to be responsive to hidden gender bias; and (ii) The regulations that prohibit officers taking informal charges should be enforced in an effort to build greater trust in the registrars and registry staff.

The Lao National Chamber of Commerce and Industry (LNCCI), in conjunction with the Lao National Commission for the Advancement of Women, Mothers and Children, should focus on: (i) developing a one-stop portal that contains the relevant information for registering a business as well as links to other resources such as financial literacy training and ICT training; and (ii) increasing awareness among micro and small businesses at the provincial level, with a focus on women entrepreneurs.

Large businesses have an important role to play in enabling smaller businesses and are doing so as part of their corporate social responsibility. They could contribute to empowering women-led and women-owned enterprises in two ways: (i) provide preference to women-led and women-owned enterprises for supply of goods and services and in doing so encourage these enterprises to become registered; and (ii) financial institutions in particular should consider the scope for developing alternative credit ratings systems that will enable women-led enterprises to access credit and grow.

Civil society has played a significant role in highlighting gender equality and can assist in developing an inclusive private sector by: (i) forming partnerships with the Ministry of Industry and Commerce and the LNCCI to engage in awareness-raising campaigns among small and micro businesses at provincial level; and (ii) advocating for increasing awareness of business registration and providing training on gender-aware policies and regulation.

Chapter 1

Introduction

It is widely recognized that gender equality can lead to improved development outcomes for families, communities, and nation states.[1] Gender equality is one of the Sustainable Development Goals (SDGs) and is endorsed by the Lao People's Democratic Republic (Lao PDR). The Asian Development Bank (ADB) is committed to this end and has stated that it will support targeted operations to empower women and girls and that at least 75% of its operations will promote gender equality by 2030.[2]

Women make up 49.9% of the population in the Lao PDR and are active participants in the 133,995 businesses that operate in the country. They often run micro and small enterprises concentrated in services, trade, and manufacturing. They operate across all provinces with the largest number of women-led enterprises based in Khammouan, Xekong, and Salavan. The need to empower women has been recognized by the Lao PDR, which has introduced laws and regulations to promote the advancement of women. This includes the 2020 promulgation of the Law on Gender Equality, which states that women and men should have economic equality. The government has committed to the objectives of the Committee on the Elimination of Discrimination against Women and has established the Lao National Commission for the Advancement of Women, Mothers and Children. The Lao Women's Union also attests to the commitment of the government to gender equality. While these efforts have seen the Lao PDR improve its position in the Global Gender Gap Index, climbing to 43rd from 52nd place in 2020, it has been noted that the implementation of equality laws and regulations remains weak.[3]

Women are more likely to operate informally, pay relatively more for registering their business, and are less likely to grow their companies relative to their male counterparts. There is a significant gender gap in enterprise ownership, with 63.5% of enterprises having male majority ownership and only 36.5% with women majority ownership. It is evident that women's effective participation in the private sector is challenged by sociocultural norms and practices that cannot be addressed by laws and regulations alone. Further, the coronavirus disease (COVID-19) has more adversely impacted women who are concentrated in tourism industries.

Since 2018, the Government of the Lao PDR has been focused on improving its business environment to facilitate investment and enterprise growth through regulatory reform. One such reform has been the Prime Minister's Order No. 02/2018 (PMO 02/2018) that aims to streamline business procedures to reduce time and costs for a more speedy, transparent, effective business climate. Such reform has the potential to promote both women-led and male-led enterprises equally. This report assesses the way this reform has impacted on enterprises. It relies on data collected for the Provincial Facilitation for Investment and Trade (ProFIT) survey that was carried out in 2017 and 2019. In 2019, a set of questions was introduced to the survey to collate select gender-disaggregated data, which has been analyzed to assess the impact on women in business and the experience of women in enterprises. This marks the first step in identifying the gendered impact of regulatory initiatives and points to ways of addressing the hidden bias that shapes policy and institutional practice. It is only by ensuring that both women and men's businesses prosper that the Lao PDR can achieve inclusive economic growth and sustained private sector development in accordance with its SDG commitments.

---

[1]   International Monetary Fund. 2018. *Pursuing Women's Economic Empowerment.* https://www.imf.org/en/Publications/Policy-Papers/Issues/2018/05/31/pp053118pursuing-womens-economic-empowerment; UN Women.

[2]   ADB. 2018. *Achieving a Prosperous, Inclusive, Resilient, and Sustainable Asia and the Pacific.* Manila. p. 15.

[3]   Government of the Lao PDR. 2021. *Voluntary National Review on the Implementation of the 2030 Agenda for Sustainable Development.* pp. 47–48.

Chapter 2

Women's Participation in Business: A Contextual Background

This section examines the legal, economic, and cultural context in which women engage with business activities. It sets the scene for the analysis of the ProFIT 2019 survey results. The discussion is carried out under three subheadings: an analysis of the laws promoting gender equality and their impact on women's enterprises; the key constraints which impinge on women's engagement in business activities; and the shape of women's enterprises in the Lao PDR. Comparable economic governance surveys and their limited focus on women's enterprises is also discussed in this section.

A.   Laws and Institutions for Gender Equality

The Lao PDR has ratified the Convention on the Elimination of all Forms of Discrimination Against Women and has adopted several laws that promote gender equality and economic participation as described in Table 1.[4]

Table 1: Summary of Gender Equality Laws

Lao PDR's Constitution of 2015 (Amended)	Article 22: States that citizens, irrespective of their sex, social status, education, faith, and ethnic group, are all equal before the law
	Article 37: Provides that citizens of both genders enjoy equal rights in political, economic, cultural, and social fields and in family affairs
	Article 7: Recognizes the Lao Women's Union as an important representative organization
Law on Development and Protection of Women, endorsed in 2004	Article 13: Gives equal rights for women and men, which means equality in self-development, including in politics, economy, society and culture, and family affairs
Decree on the Building and Development of Labour Skills No. 036/PM of 2010	Article 3: States that every Lao worker, both female and male, regardless of ethnic group, has an equal right to have their labor skills developed
Law on Labour of 2013	Article 96: Provides for gender equality in employment in which women have the rights to work and have a career in all manufacturing and service businesses that do not conflict with the law
Law on Combatting and Preventing Violence Against Women of 2015	Article 2: Recognizes the need to prevent violence that is likely to result in physical, psychological, sexual, or economic suffering to women
2020 Promulgation of the Law on Gender Equality	Article 10: States that women and men have economic equality such as in terms of access to economic resources, labor market, employment, training, and welfare benefits
	Article 23: States that gender equality is the empowerment of women through providing opportunities for their education, training, and development, ensuring that they shall receive equal benefits to men in the same conditions

Lao PDR = Lao People's Democratic Republic.
Source: Compiled by Asian Development Bank staff based on the *Lao Official Gazette*, Ministry of Justice (laoofficialgazette.gov.la).

---

4   Other gender equality laws that do not deal directly with economic participation have not been included in this table. They include the Law on Family, Law on Anti-Trafficking in Persons, and Law on Protection of the Rights and Interests of Children.

It has been recognized that the introduction of these laws demonstrates that significant progress has been made toward meeting the SDGs, in particular SDG 5 on gender equality.[5] As reported by the World Economic Forum, progress toward gender parity has been made on several fronts. Women's share in the National Assembly increased to 27.5% in 2019, which was above the global average of 24.5%; gender parity at primary school level has been tracking well for both girls and boys; and women are occupying more senior and managerial roles.[6]

However, the gender gap remains in many areas, particularly in relation to economic participation and paid employment. The same World Economic Forum study recognized the gender gap in enterprise ownership, noting that while 63.5% of enterprises had male majority ownership, only 36.5% had female majority ownership.[7] It also noted that women receive 10% lower earnings on average than their male counterparts in similar occupations and locations, and with similar qualifications, in the private sector.[8] It has also been reported that 61% of women work with their families for no pay, compared with 25% of males, which means that women have less time to commit to paid activities.[9] Furthermore, while women's share in the National Assembly increased, they only hold a small fraction of leadership positions at the provincial level, making up only 2.4% of village chiefs and 11.8% of deputy village chiefs. Likewise, women hold fewer decision-making positions in government, reported at 31% and constituting merely 17% of directors general of departments within ministries.[10]

The need to promote private sector activities in the Lao PDR has seen the introduction of laws and policies on enterprise development. But these regulations do not make any reference to women's businesses or make special provision for their needs.[11] Of note is PMO 02/2018, aimed at the improvement of regulations and coordination mechanisms on doing business by streamlining registration procedures through the simultaneous issue of the enterprise certificate and TIN.[12] This has been an important reform requiring government at all levels to simplify the issuance of registration certification to start business activities. In addition to the announced reforms, the government has been reviewing regulations for business operating licenses and considering risk-based approaches to licensing reform.[13] Streamlining the administration and procedures of business certifications, licenses and permits, is noted as an important priority in the coming years.[14] To date, the impact of these initiatives on women's businesses has not been assessed, with the exception of the ProFIT 2019 survey, analyzed in Chapter 3 of this report.

An institutional framework for promoting gender equality has been established with the Lao National Commission for the Advancement of Women, Mothers and Children, which has responsibility for monitoring the implementation of gender-related strategies and action plans at national, provincial,

---

[5]   Footnote 3, p. 6.

[6]   World Economic Forum. 2021. *Global Gender Gap Report 2021*. Geneva. p. 24 https://www3.weforum.org/docs/WEF_GGGR_2021.pdf.

[7]   Footnote 6 p. 248.

[8]   World Bank. 2020. *Lao People's Democratic Republic Poverty Assessment 2020: Catching Up and Falling Behind*. Washington, DC. p. 92. https://openknowledge.worldbank.org/handle/10986/34528.

[9]   United Nations Convention on the Elimination of All Forms of Discrimination Against Women. 2018. *List of issues and questions in relation to the combined eighth and ninth periodic reports of the Lao People's Democratic Republic*. p. 8.

[10] Footnote 3, pp. 47–48.

[11] See: Law on the Promotion and Development of Small and Medium-Sized Enterprises, endorsed in 2011; Small and Medium Enterprises Development Plan 2016–2020, a policy which was endorsed by Prime Minister's Decree No. 253/PM on 18 January 2017; and 2019 ProFIT report.

[12] See: 2019 ProFIT report.

[13] Jacobs, Cordova, and Associates. *Component A2: Streamlining and Publishing Business Operating Licenses*. p. 4.

[14] World Bank. 2021. *Annual Implementation Progress Report (January–December 2021) and Priorities for FY 2022: Lao PDR Competitiveness and Trade Project*. Washington, DC. p. 14.

district, and village levels, while the Lao Women's Union is charged with promoting gender equality within the family structure. This institution has advocated for a policy to mandate that 30% of leadership positions should be occupied by women. The government has applied temporary special measures to promote gender equality in all fields of decision-making and is advised by the National Commission for the Advancement of Women on how to fulfill its obligations under international treaties.[15] In October 2020, the vice-president of the Lao Women's Union, Her Excellency Bouachanh Syhanath, affirmed the government's commitment to the Beijing Declaration and Platform for Action and the 2030 Agenda for Sustainable Development, pointing to building women's entrepreneurship and women's enterprises as one of the top five priorities for the 5 years.[16] However, little data are currently available on their efforts at enabling women's participation in the private sector and on how they assist in overcoming cultural norms and institutional bias, which impact adversely on women's involvement in business.

Promoting gender equality does not rely solely on governments. The private sector has been recognized as an important driver of gender equality in developing countries, as seen from the example of over 5,000 companies that are signatories to the Women's Empowerment Principles, which includes 15 companies based in the Lao PDR.[17] Some of these companies have introduced policies to promote and retain women staff. One example is Phoubia Mining Company, which has instituted a policy requiring that at least 20% of the total staff are women. In other countries, companies have adopted women-friendly procurement policies with the intent of encouraging women-owned businesses.[18] There is potential for financial institutions, eight of which have signed the Women's Empowerment Principles in the Lao PDR, to drive gender equality by ensuring financial access for women entrepreneurs.[19]

B.   Key Constraints to Women's Effective Participation

Women face many hurdles when seeking to engage in the private sector. All these hurdles are buttressed by social norms and cultural practices that dictate how much autonomy a woman has and how much energy and time she can afford to business activities. These sociocultural norms shape the interpretation of laws, regulations, and policies and they also determine the response of organizations, which can have the effect of being inclusive or discriminatory.

Sociocultural norms can have a negative impact on women's engagement with the formal economy, which in turn has a negative impact on the development of the private sector. Private sector development is associated with higher taxes and government revenue, formal jobs that can guarantee social protection such as health insurance and leave provisions, and investor confidence which can direct investment into growth industries—all of which remains untapped. The constraints faced by women have been described in five interrelated categories.

---

[15] Committee on the Elimination of Discrimination against Women. 2017. *Consideration of reports submitted by States parties under Article 18 of the Convention. Combined eighth and ninth periodic reports of States parties due in 2014 Lao People's Democratic Republic.* https://tbinternet.ohchr.org/Treaties/CEDAW/Shared%20Documents/LAO/CEDAW_C_LAO_8-9_5963_E.pdf.

[16] Permanent Mission of the Lao People's Democratic Republic to the United Nations. 2020. *Statement by H.E. Mrs. Bouachanh Syhanath, Vice-President of Lao Women's Union, at the High-level meeting on the twenty-fifth anniversary of the Fourth World Conference on Women (BEIJING+25).* https://www.un.int/lao/statements_speeches/statement-he-mrs-bouachanh-syhanath-vice-president-lao-women%E2%80%99s-union-high-level.

[17] Women's Empowerment Principles. *WEPs Signatories.* https://www.weps.org/companies.

[18] ADB. 2018. *Emerging Lessons on Women's Entrepreneurship in Asia and the Pacific.* Manila. p. 39. https://www.adb.org/publications/women-entrepreneurship-lessons-asia-pacific.

[19] Footnote 18, pp. 8, 21.

Inequitable impact of sociocultural norms. The vice-president of the Lao National Chamber of Commerce and Industry (LNCCI) has referred the impact of sociocultural norms, noting that women had to be brave to undertake business as they faced security risks when traveling alone, which made running a business all the more challenging. Women are more vulnerable than men to violence and trafficking, which impedes their autonomy and agency. This has been recognized by the government, as demonstrated by the legal reforms initiated and the strategies developed to meet SDG 5.[20]

The Lao PDR has the highest proportion of early marriage and the highest adolescent birth rate among the Association of Southeast Asian Nations (ASEAN) countries. It has been reported that 23.5% of girls aged between 15 and 19 are currently married. This impacts on their ability to improve their education or to engage in business activities.[21] As primary carers for children and elderly family members, women take on greater responsibilities at home, which impinges on their ability to work. It was acknowledged by an interviewee, the general manager of a private company, that women have an important role in preserving culture and ensuring that their families are healthy. Women spend over four times the number of hours on unpaid care work compared to men, leaving them less time to focus on business.[22] They also have to juggle work and caring activities and it was reported that women's businesses were more likely to be home-based to facilitate caring activities, whereas men's businesses were much more likely to be mobile (Table 2).

Table 2: Location of Household Head's Business

Business Operations	Household Head (number)			Household Head (% share)		
	Male	Female	Total	Male	Female	Total
Home residence	101,812	21,371	123,183	47.9	10.1	58.0
Industrial site	1,664	0	1,664	0.8	0.0	0.8
Traditional market	29,439	3,917	33,356	13.9	1.8	15.7
Shop	4,933	147	5,080	2.3	0.1	2.4
Roadside	16,165	3,869	20,034	7.6	1.8	9.4
Other fixed place	7,715	8,36	8,551	3.6	0.4	4.0
Mobile	16,596	3,935	20,531	7.8	1.9	9.7
Total	**178,324**	**34,075**	**212,399**	**84.0**	**16.0**	**100.0**

Source: Asian Development Bank staff calculations from the Lao People's Democratic Republic Expenditure and Consumption Survey 2018.

Social norms restrict women's ability to attend social networking events and benefit from professional connections.[23] They can impede certain business activities, such as traveling long distances for work.[24] Three of the interviewees recognized the limits on women engaging freely in social activities, especially in activities involving alcohol consumption, which they viewed as important to networking and possible business opportunities. One interviewee went on to suggest that any implementation of government initiatives was likely to have limited effect as society still does not accept businesswomen, reiterating the limits of regulations to change sociocultural norms.

---

[20] Footnote 3, p. 19.
[21] Footnote 3, p. 50.
[22] United Nations Children's Fund (UNICEF). 2021. *Impact of COVID-19 on Reimagining Gender*. https://lao.unfpa.org/sites/default/files/pub-pdf/covid-19_impact_assessment_lao_pdr-_brief_gender.pdf.
[23] Lao Business Women's Survey, 2018.
[24] ADB and the World Bank. *Lao Gender Assessment*. p. 41. https://openknowledge.worldbank.org/handle/10986/16511?show=full.

Lack of access to finance. Less than 10% of enterprises reported having a loan in the last 3 years,[25] with lower prevalence among women-headed enterprises (Table 3). Women report that complicated lending procedures, lack of collateral, and lack of a track record act as deterrents (footnote 23). Although women are reputedly good savers, making up 61% of microfinance savers nationally, few are able to obtain commercial bank loans.[26] It was reported that 61.4% of women relied on the village fund or relatives for finance compared to 36.8% of men.[27]

Table 3: Enterprises with Access to Finance

Business Registration	% Share		
	Men-Led	Women-Led	Total
Loans in the past 3 years	10.4	9.0	9.6
No loans in the past 3 years	89.6	91.0	90.4

Source: Asian Development Bank staff calculations from Lao Statistics Bureau, 2020 Economic Census.

There is evidence to support the conclusion that women have been able to run successful and profitable businesses across Asia. However across ASEAN economies, only 5%-6% of microenterprises, 12%–15% of small firms, and 17%–21% of medium-sized enterprises had adequate access to finance.[28] Many women who run micro and small businesses lack knowledge about the types of collateral and often do not have business plans or complete business registrations, which is necessary for being eligible for credit from commercial banks. Land, which is the most common form of collateral in developed countries, is rarely used in the Lao PDR due to customary communal ownership rules, social norms, and the practice of financial institutions. Women often use their husband's name to take out a loan or resort to microfinance organizations and informal money lenders, which generally charge extremely high interest rates that make businesses unsustainable.[29]

Limited access to networks and markets. Networks are defined as a group of interconnected people and can include professional networks, business networks, and trade networks. The mandate provided to the Lao Women's Union, which is a network of employees, shows the crucial role they can play in seeking recognition and support for specific issues. The Lao PDR has several such networks that support micro and small enterprises and the Lao Business Women's Association is one that is focused on women's entrepreneurship. While a national network is likely to advocate well on equality issues, it is also less likely to cater for the specific needs of women entrepreneurs who may benefit from training in their fields and collaborating with others in their sectors. New networks aimed at women entrepreneurs may be necessary in such circumstances.

Access to markets was reported as a major constraint in the 2020 Economic Census by one in three women (footnote 25). Physically accessing markets away from home may not be easy for women in the Lao PDR. It was noted that few women either own or can drive a car and that only 5% of women can operate a car compared to 48% of men. Accessing online markets also poses a challenge as 94.6%

---

[25] Lao Economic Census III (2019–2020).

[26] R. Keovialey. 2018. *Overview of Women's Entrepreneurship in Micro, Small and Medium Enterprises in Lao PDR.* pp. 10–11.

[27] Law Economic Statistics, See Gender Cross Tabs that Mai prepared on 5 Nov – under Access to Finance tab.

[28] ADB. 2018. *Emerging Lessons on Women's Entrepreneurship in Asia and the Pacific: Case Studies from the Asian Development Bank and The Asia Foundation.* Manila. October. p 8. https://www.adb.org/sites/default/files/publication/459551/women-entrepreneurship-lessons-asia-pacific.pdf.

[29] Footnote 27, p. 11.

of women-led enterprises have reported that they do not have any familiarity with using information and communication technology (ICT) compared to 91.8% of men-led enterprises (Table 4).

Table 4: Usage of ICT Tools in a Business
(% of enterprises)

Usage	% Share		
	Men-led	Women-led	Total
Use ICT	8.2	5.4	6.6
Do not use ICT	91.8	94.6	93.4

ICT = information and communication technology.
Source: Asian Development Bank staff calculations from the Lao Statistics Bureau's Economic Census 2020.

Inadequate access to education and skills training. Skills in product development, business management, and navigating the financial requirements of banks are often reported as challenging by women entrepreneurs globally.[30] The origin of this skills shortage is the high school dropout rate of girls by the age of 16, with only 19.2% of girls in the Lao PDR still attending school when aged 17–25, compared to 24.8% of males.[31] Women repeatedly reported lower knowledge of ICT equipment and ICT use. Although it is reported that both women and men use the internet in similar ways, in 2020 the economic census reported that only 2.2% of women-headed enterprises used ICT to sell their products and services compared to 3.3% of men. Likewise, more women ran their businesses without any technological assistance compared to their male counterparts.[32]

Cost of compliance. The cost of engaging in the formal economy cannot be underestimated. Literature on women's entrepreneurship points to women's preference to operate in the informal economy. The reasons include the need to manage family responsibilities and the pressure of conforming to sociocultural norms.[33] It has been reported that 65% of women decided to start a business because they were unable to find another source of income, compared to 34% of men, which suggests that their preparedness for the task may not be sufficient.[34] Further, the time taken to formalize, and the costs involved including registration and license fees and taxes, act as deterrents to entering the formal private sector. A further challenge is reported in the Lao Business Women's survey, which includes the costs resulting from racketeering and bribes. Such costs, when coupled with sociocultural norms, are likely to have a greater adverse impact on women's businesses. Women reported that they were less likely to follow the tax system, which could be a result of less awareness and inadequate records.

[30] ADB. 2018. *Emerging Lessons on Women's Entrepreneurship in Asia and the Pacific*. Manila. pp. 10–11.
[31] Government of the Lao PDR, Ministry of Planning and Investment. 2020. *Window of Opportunity for Realizing a Demographic Dividend*. Vientiane: MPI. p. 3. https://lao.unfpa.org/sites/default/files/pub-pdf/dd_brief_eng.pdf.
[32] Lao Economic Census III (2019–2020); Government of the Lao PDR. 2021. *Voluntary National Review on the Implementation of the 2030 Agenda for Sustainable Development*. p. 48. https://sustainabledevelopment.un.org/content/documents/279472021_VNR_Report_Lao.pdf.
[33] S. T. Karki, M. Xheneti, and A. Madden. 2021. To Formalize or Not to Formalize: Women Entrepreneurs' Sensemaking of Business Registration in the Context of Nepal. *Journal of Business Ethics*. Vol. 173. pp. 687–708.
[34] Government of the Lao PDR, Ministry of Industry and Commerce (MOIC). 2020. *Lao PDR Gender Study*. Vientiane: MOIC. p. 8.

C.   The Shape of Women's Enterprises

Women make up 49.9% of the population and are active participants in both the formal and informal economies. A World Bank survey reported that women are engaged in diverse informal businesses both in urban and rural areas including retail (e.g., phone and computer sales); manufacturing (furniture and metal products); and professional services (e.g., transport provision). However, in enterprises throughout the country, women are more likely to be engaged in business activities in micro and small enterprises than men (Figure 1).

Figure 1: Enterprises' Leadership by Gender

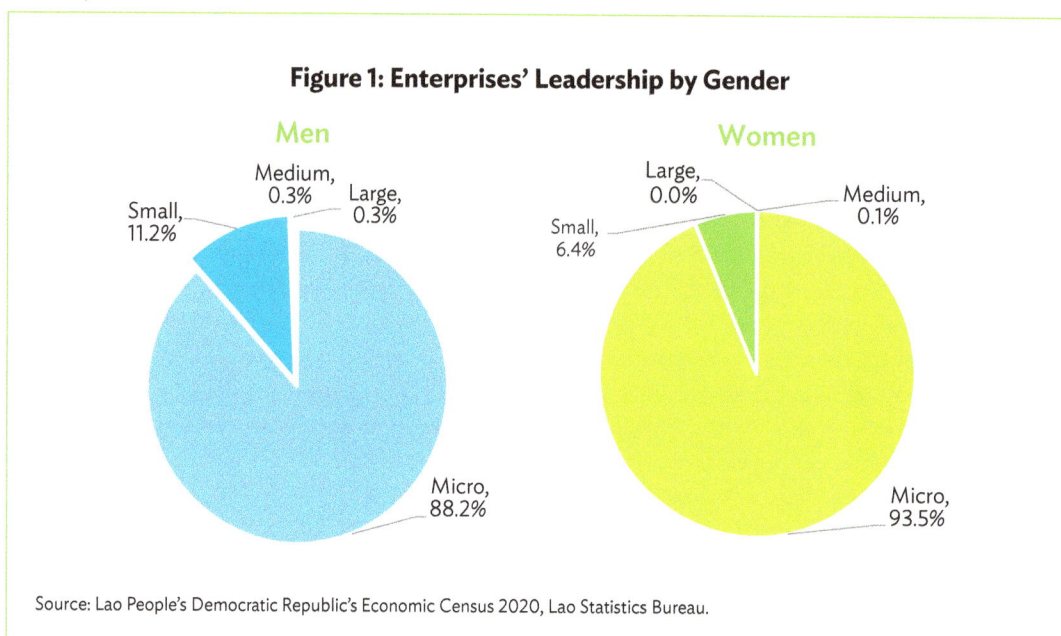

Source: Lao People's Democratic Republic's Economic Census 2020, Lao Statistics Bureau.

There were 133,995 businesses operating in 2020, of which 69.6% were unregistered (Table 5). A study conducted by the Ministry of Industry and Commerce listed six reasons for not proceeding with registration (Table 6). As seen from the table, the biggest difference between the responses of women-owned and men-owned enterprises was the bribes they stated that registered businesses need to pay. While 36% of women-owned businesses stated this as a reason for not registering a business, only 22% of men-owned enterprises considered this to be a reason. More women-owned businesses reported the time, fees and paperwork involved as a reason for not registering a business compared to male-owned enterprises.

Table 5: Business Registration
(% of enterprises)

Business Registration	% Share		
	Men-Led	Women-Led	Total
With business certificate	34.0	27.6	30.4
Without business certificate	66.0	72.4	69.6

Source: Lao People's Democratic Republic's Economic Census 2020, Lao Statistics Bureau.

Table 6: Reasons for Not Registering a Business
(% of enterprises)

Reason	Women-Owned Enterprises	Male-Owned Enterprises
No benefit in registering	76	69
Lack of information about the process of registration and information on where to register	51	78
Time, fees, and paperwork (%)	51	38
Taxes levied if registered	42	31
Inspections and meetings with government	36	24
Bribes that registered businesses need to pay	36	22

Source: Ministry of Industry and Commerce. 2020. *Lao PDR Gender Study*. p. 11.

To transition from the informal to the formal economy, businesses are required to have an enterprise registration certificate, a business operating license, and a TIN. Recent data show that women-led enterprises are less likely to meet each of these requirements than men-led enterprises (Table 5). It also shows that only 1.7% of enterprises participate in social security or pension schemes for employees, with fewer women-led enterprises doing so (Table 7).

Table 7: Type of Social Pension Scheme
(% of enterprises)

Type of Social Scheme	% Share		
	Men-Led	Women-Led	Total
With social pension scheme	2.2	1.3	1.7
State social security	1.0	0.3	0.6
Private social security	1.2	0.9	1.1
Without social pension scheme	97.8	98.7	98.3

Source: Lao People's Democratic Republic's Economic Census 2020, Lao Statistics Bureau.

Such consistent noncompliance suggests that the benefits of formalization are either not evident or not widely understood. The benefits include access to credit, networks, and business development support, which in turn encourages the development of the formal economy, the growth of businesses, and the expansion of government revenues. These benefits are outweighed by the costs of formalization, which includes expenses in terms of time and informal payments for obtaining a registration certificate, licenses, permits, and paying tax.

Registration certifies the formal establishment of a legal entity, which can take the form of a sole trader, partnership, state-owned enterprise, and private or public company; and is granted by the provincial government. Although there are more enterprises owned and operated by women (56.3% of all enterprises), only one in four women had a registration certificate, compared with one in three for men (footnote 25). More women find it easier to operate informally than men.

A sector business operating license is also required by the government. Only 16.9% of the women-headed enterprises had obtained a business license, compared with 28.5% of men-led businesses.[35] Therefore, enterprises headed by women were less likely to have a sector business operating than enterprises headed by men. In addition, all registered enterprises are required to apply for a tax registration certificate and obtain a TIN. Women-led enterprises had lower compliance, with 10.9% being women-led enterprises stating that they had a TIN compared with 15.5% being men-led enterprises.

Women-led enterprises operate across all provinces in the Lao PDR, with the largest numbers based in Khammouan, Xekong, and Salavan. The most popular business type is a private enterprise, and 99.4% of women-led enterprises and 97.1% of male-led enterprises utilized this form. This is consistent with evidence across Asia and the Pacific where the majority of businesses are sole traders and are likely to be micro and small enterprises.[36] Women's enterprises are concentrated in three main areas: trade, manufacturing, and hotels and restaurants (Table 8).

Table 8: Three Main Sectors of Activity

Sector	% Share		
	Men-Led	Women-Led	Total
Trade (wholesale and retail)	26.3	37.5	63.8
Manufacturing	6.9	7.1	14.1
Hotels and restaurants	3.2	7.6	10.8
Other sectors	7.3	4.0	11.4

Source: Lao People's Democratic Republic's Economic Census 2020, Lao Statistics Bureau.

The Lao PDR's formal economy has undergone significant changes in recent times, which have had an adverse impact on women's businesses and their employment. The growth of the investment in hydropower and mining industries over the last decade was coupled with a downturn in the nonfarm private sector, particularly impacting on the manufacturing and construction enterprises. It resulted in 30,000 enterprises exiting, reducing the total number from 163,000 in 2012 to 133,000 in 2019.[37] It is estimated that 7% of micro and small enterprises exited each year during this period, while the exit rate among larger enterprises was lower at 3.7% per year for these years.[38] Among the businesses that discontinued their operations in 2018, 40% were fully owned by women. Women's labor force participation has also dropped significantly: between 2012 and 2019 this participation decreased by 15.8% (from 81.8% to 66%), compared to a 9% drop in male participation (from 87.4% to 78.4%).[39]

This has been exacerbated by the challenges posed by COVID-19, which has taken its toll on the services sector, including enterprises supplying hospitality, tourism, and transport services. Women

---

[35]   The total number of enterprises in the survey was 133,995. See: Lao Economic Census III (2019–2020).

[36]   ADB. 2014. *Gender Tool Kit: Micro, Small and Medium-Sized Enterprise Finance and Development*. Manila. p. 3. https://www.adb.org/documents/gender-tool-kit-micro-small-and-medium-sized-enterprise-finance-and-development.

[37]   World Bank Note 2021. p. 7.

[38]   Footnote 37, p. 8.

[39]   World Bank. 2020. *Lao People's Democratic Republic Poverty Assessment 2020: Catching Up and Falling Behind*. Washington, DC. p. 58. https://openknowledge.worldbank.org/handle/10986/34528.

have been disproportionately impacted due to their participation in the hardest-hit sectors, trade and services.[40]

D.   Comparative Economic Governance Surveys and Gender

Economic governance indexes have been used as a tool to assess aspects of regulatory governance in various countries, including Viet Nam, which is relevant to this analysis. Viet Nam measures economic governance of their provinces, aimed at identifying regulatory constraints to growth. The indicators measure the responses of firms to 10 components of governance including entry costs for business start-ups, time requirements for bureaucratic procedures and inspections, informal charges paid by firms, transparency in decision-making processes, and favoritism exhibited by government to specific groups. However, neither of these country reports considers the challenges women encounter when engaging in the private sector or the gendered impacts of regulatory approaches and institutional practices. Reforms undertaken and policies implemented because of these studies hold critical lessons for the Lao PDR as it reflects on policy initiatives to reshape its private sector.

The Viet Nam report, which is the *16th Provincial Competitiveness Index Report*, scores the reaction to governance reforms of more than 8,000 private businesses across 63 provinces.[41] It reported amid the COVID-19 crisis with clear evidence of the adverse impact of the pandemic on business. This report shows a steady improvement in how business viewed the provincial authorities' flexibility in creating an enabling environment for the private sector. It also demonstrates that businesses were supportive of the efforts to fight against corruption and informal charges.[42] However, it reported businesses were dissatisfied with a number of other administrative procedures including payment of taxes, while social insurance and applying for a license remained burdensome, requiring further reform.[43]

The Myanmar report, initiated in 2018 and published for the second time in 2020, is based on the responses of 5,605 businesses across the country.[44] Unlike Viet Nam, these businesses were not required to pay informal charges such as bribes for business entry, although it was reported that such payments were needed to receive construction certificates and to win procurement contracts.[45] A reform initiated was the one-stop shop for administrative processes. It was reported that by 2020, such one-stop shops had been introduced into all townships and it was observed that the people occupying these desks were helpful and that having resources such as computers, fax machines, and hard copies of documents were necessary for their efficient functioning.[46]

While these reports provide significant information on the regulatory environment and give examples of successful policy initiatives, the lack of a gender analysis is a significant shortcoming.

---

[40]   World Bank. 2021. *Lao PDR Economic Monitor: A Path to Recovery*. p. 53. https://pubdocs.worldbank.org/en/147871629861334356/Lao-PDR-Economic-Monitor-August-2021.

[41]   E. Malesky, P. T. Ngoc, and P. N. Thach. 2021. *The Vietnam Provincial Competitiveness Index: Measuring Economic Governance for Private Sector Development, 2020 Final Report*. Vietnam Chamber of Commerce and Industry and United States Agency for International Development. Ha Noi. (Referred to as *The Vietnam Provincial Competitiveness Index Report*.)

[42]   Footnote 41, pp. 27–28.

[43]   Footnote 41, p. 29.

[44]   E. J. Malesky, D. Dulay, and V. Peltovuori. 2020. *The Myanmar Business Environment Index: Measuring Economic Governance for Private Sector Development*. The DaNa Facility and The Asia Foundation. Yangon, Myanmar. (Referred to as *The Myanmar Business Environment Index Report*.)

[45]   Footnote 44, p. 14, 42.

[46]   Footnote 47, p. 13.

Chapter 3

ProFIT Survey

A. Methodology and Respondent Profiles

1. Methodology

In 2019, survey data were collected from 1,357 enterprises in 17 provinces across the Lao PDR. The survey collected data on indicators which were then consolidated in six subindexes. The six subindexes are (i) starting a business, (ii) transparency and access to information, (iii) regulatory burden, (iv) informal charges, (v) consistency in policy implementation, and (vi) business friendliness of the provincial administration (Figure 2). The introductory questions asked respondents to provide general information on their businesses, including type, size, gender of the chief executive officer (CEO), and professional background. It required respondents to provide specific numerical answers regarding costs, times, and other indicators (Appendix 2).

Figure 2: ProFIT Index Components

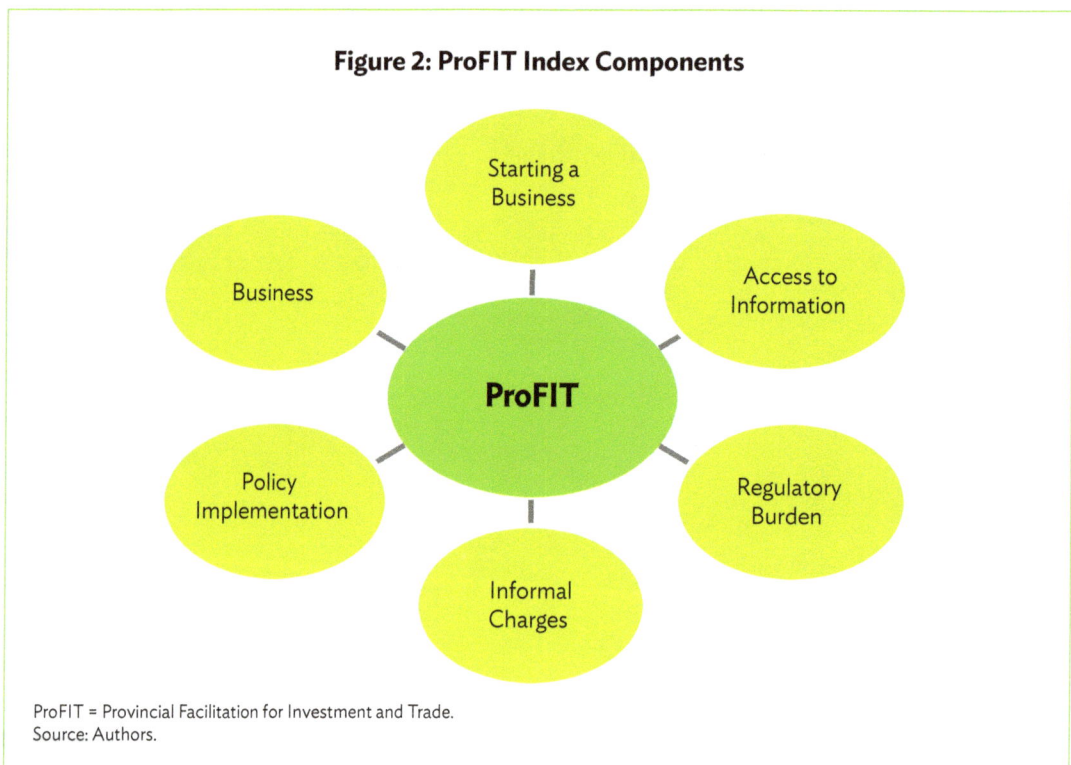

ProFIT = Provincial Facilitation for Investment and Trade.
Source: Authors.

The study team of this report ensured that at least 60 business owners responded in each province. Approximately 60% of the enterprises attended a ProFIT 2019 survey workshop, conducted from 1 October to 6 November 2019. At the ProFIT workshops, CEOs of the selected enterprises completed a questionnaire and were invited to share their views on the challenges and opportunities in their local business environments. The LNCCI sent online versions of the questionnaire to business owners who could not attend the workshops in person. The enterprises that participated in the ProFIT 2019 survey represented approximately 1% of all enterprises as of 2020, with provincial variation from 0.5% in Louangphabang and 4% in Xekong. For the first time, the questionnaire included two questions on gender as follows:

(i)   A question about the sex of the CEO—where the CEO was a woman, the business was defined as a women-owned enterprise, and

(ii)   A question on the sex of the owners of the enterprise—where women's shareholding was at least 30% the business was defined as a women-owned enterprise.[47]

It aimed to extract gender-disaggregated data and calculate the ProFIT scores by gender of women-led and men-led enterprises as well as women-owned and men-owned enterprises. It allowed exploration of the subindexes and their component indicators to reveal gender differences between enterprises.[48] Gender-disaggregated data were collected at a level that allowed for results to be analyzed at the national level only. The responses to each of the six subindexes is discussed, following an assessment of the respondents' profiles. In addition, as there are substantial differences in the ownership and leadership of enterprises by firm size across genders, with women overrepresented in micro-firm classifications. Selected data are therefore reported at a disaggregate level by enterprise size.

2.   Scoring Methodology

The ProFIT index is made up of six subindexes, each with an equal weight of 16.7% of the total score (Table 9). Each subindex is computed based on responses on several questions from the questionnaire. Answers to each question in the survey were scored from 0 to 100 points, with 0 as the lowest or worst and 100 as the highest or the best, and provincial results were measured against a perfect score to arrive at each province's "distance to the frontier." Extreme outliers were eliminated from the data set before the survey results were tabulated.

Table 9: Methodology for Computing the 2019 ProFIT Index

Subindex	%	Indicator	%
1. Starting a business	100	Business registration time	50
		Business registration cost	50
2. Transparency and access to information	100	Access to provincial documents	60
		Provincial websites	20
		Opportunity to comment on draft regulations	20
3. Regulatory burden	100	Inspections by authorities	30
		Tax registration certificate renewal time	35
		Tax registration certificate renewal cost	35
4. Informal charges	100	Informal charges as a share of revenue	40
		Acceptability of informal charges	15
		Commonality of tax negotiations	15
		Necessity of informal charges	15
		Public disclosure of formal charges	15

continued on next page

---

[47]   The 2017 ProFIT survey did not ask these questions.

[48]   In the ProFIT survey, companies are defined as: (i) ordinary partnership, (ii) limited liability partnership, (iii) public company, (iv) limited company, and (v) others (for example, small and microenterprises).

Table 9 *continued*

Subindex	%	Indicator	%
5. Consistency of implementation	100	Advantages of personal connections	20
		Favoritism for state-owned enterprises	20
		Consistency of regulations with national rules	20
		Internal coordination to support business	20
		Provincial regulations differ from national ones	20
6. Business friendliness	100	Attitude of provincial government	25
		Helpfulness of provincial government	25
		Application of new solutions to solve problems	25
		Knowledge of Degree 02	25

ProFIT = Provincial Facilitation for Investment and Trade.
Source: Authors.

3.   Respondent Profiles

Figure 3 shows that 43% of enterprises are owned by women (defined as at least 30% of ownership is by women) compared to men with 57% of enterprises. The difference is greater when it comes to leadership within these enterprises. Only 36% of enterprises are led by women (defined as having a woman CEO) while 64% are men-led enterprises, leaving a gap of 17%. This gap is larger at 22% in enterprises led and owned by women and those led and owned by men: 28% of enterprises are women-led and women-owned, compared to 49% that are men-led and men-owned.

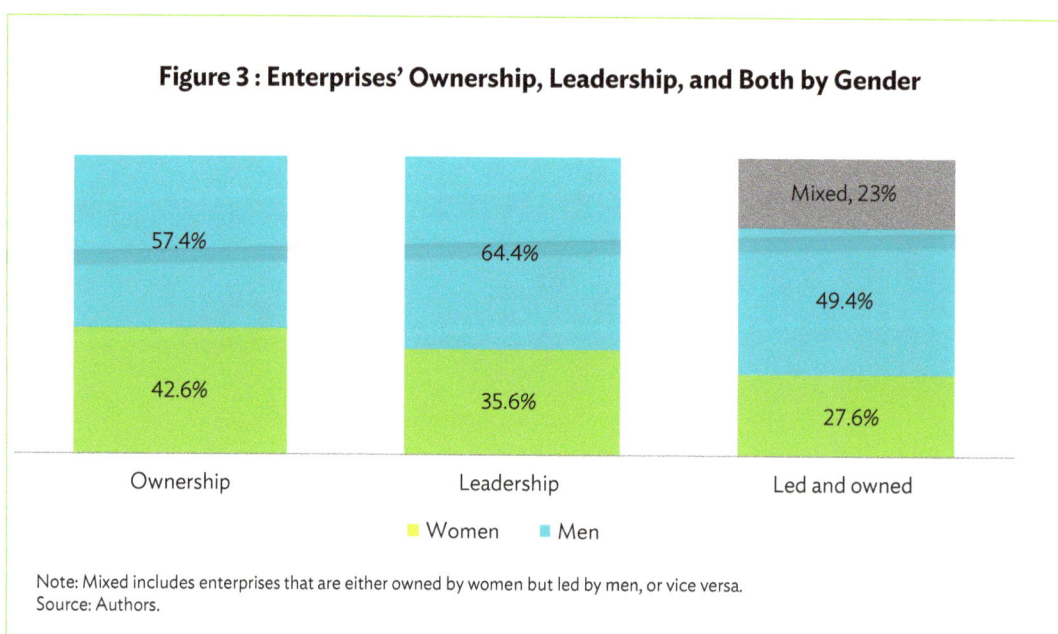

Figure 3 : Enterprises' Ownership, Leadership, and Both by Gender

Ownership: Women 42.6%, Men 57.4%
Leadership: Women 35.6%, Men 64.4%
Led and owned: Women 27.6%, Men 49.4%, Mixed 23%

■ Women   ■ Men

Note: Mixed includes enterprises that are either owned by women but led by men, or vice versa.
Source: Authors.

Across the sample, leadership and ownership by men dominated in all sectors, with the biggest gaps in construction and manufacturing. Leadership and ownership by women in enterprises is concentrated in the trade, services, and agriculture sectors, although they are still fewer than their male counterparts (Figure 4). As the data do not show the dynamics of control within these enterprises, it is not possible to conclude whether ownership equates to control, or whether the owner may indeed be a silent party, with limited rights to control the functioning of the enterprise.

The sample includes a higher share of women-led microenterprises, representing 45.1% of the total women's enterprises compared to 30.8% of men-led microenterprises (Figure 5). In addition, the sample includes more men-led enterprises that are larger in size. The three main areas of activity for micro and small enterprises are in services, trade, and manufacturing. Women-led enterprises focus on these three sectors (services, manufacturing, and trade); while the men-led enterprises are in services, manufacturing, and construction. The median number of full-time workers in women-led enterprises was six, whereas this number in men-led enterprises was 10, explained by the larger number of men-led enterprises that are operating and most likely require a larger workforce.

Figure 4: Women-Led and Men-Led Enterprises by Sector

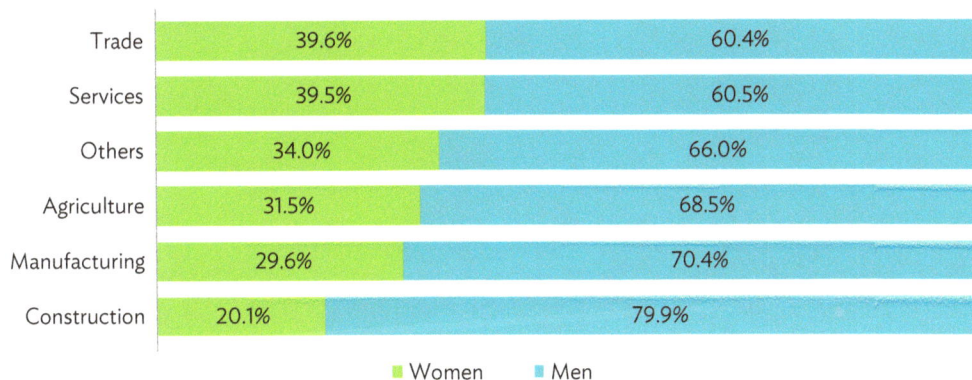

Sector	Women	Men
Trade	39.6%	60.4%
Services	39.5%	60.5%
Others	34.0%	66.0%
Agriculture	31.5%	68.5%
Manufacturing	29.6%	70.4%
Construction	20.1%	79.9%

■ Women ■ Men

Source: Authors.

Figure 5: Women-Led and Men-Led Enterprises by Size

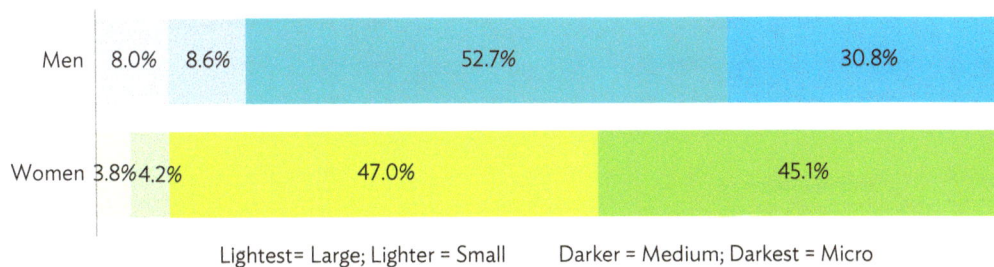

Men	8.0%	8.6%	52.7%	30.8%
Women	3.8%	4.2%	47.0%	45.1%

Lightest= Large; Lighter = Small   Darker = Medium; Darkest = Micro

Notes:
1. In the Provincial Facilitation for Investment and Trade survey, enterprises are categorized by the number of workers: a microenterprise is defined as having 1–5 workers, a small enterprise as having between 6–50 workers, a medium enterprise as having between 51–99 workers, and a large enterprise as having 100 workers or more.
2. Also see: Prime Minister's Decree No. 25, dated 16 January 2017, on the categories of small and medium-sized enterprises.
Source: Authors.

B. Result of ProFIT 2019 from a Gender Perspective

1. Scores of Women and Men in Enterprises

Figure 6 shows the scores of women and men in enterprises on the 2019 ProFIT survey across its six subindexes, including scores for leadership and ownership by sex. The score for women-led enterprises was 56.7 points out of 100, whereas men-led enterprises scored 54.8. Women-led enterprises scored higher than men-led enterprises in all subindexes except transparency and access to information. However, these scores are still relatively low, indicating significant room for improvement in the business environment. When categorized by ownership, women-owned enterprises also scored higher than men-owned enterprises at 56.38 and 53.90, respectively. Women-owned enterprises scored higher on all subindexes except on consistency of implementation.

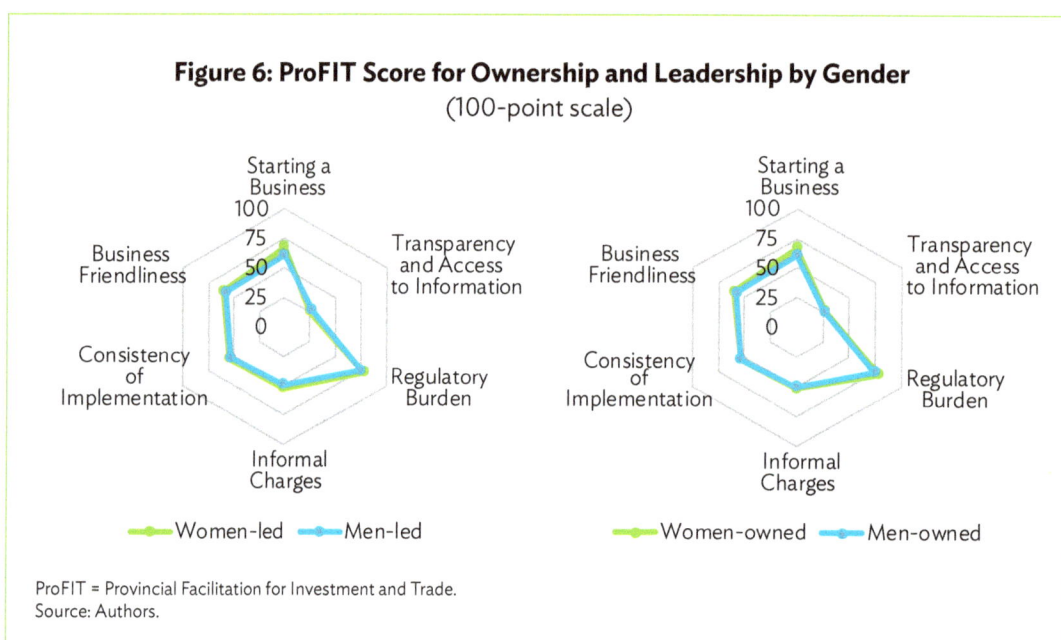

Figure 6: ProFIT Score for Ownership and Leadership by Gender
(100-point scale)

ProFIT = Provincial Facilitation for Investment and Trade.
Source: Authors.

2. Starting a Business

The starting a business subindex measures the time taken and financial expenses needed to register a business. Significant concern had been expressed on the inordinate length of time taken to register a business.[49] Between 2017 and 2019, the ProFIT survey found that there had been an improvement in the time and costs in registering a business across provinces in the Lao PDR. Figure 7 presents scores of the 2019 survey on this subindex. For leadership and ownership, the results show that women-led and women-owned enterprises scored comparatively better than their male counterparts. Women-led enterprises scored of 67.7 compared to male-led enterprises with a score of 60.5 out of a total of 100. Women-owned enterprises scored of 66.9 compared to male-owned enterprises with a score of 60.4. This is partly explained by the fact men-led and men-owned enterprises reported higher costs and more time for obtaining an enterprise registration certificate due to enterprise size and operating sector which may likely have resulted in a lower score (Figure 8).

---

49   See, for example: World Economic Forum. 2019. *Lao Country Profile on Global Competitiveness Report 2019.* http://reports. weforum.org/global-competitiveness-report-2019/economy-profiles/#economy=LAO.

Figure 7: Starting a Business for Ownership and Leadership by Gender
(100-point scale)

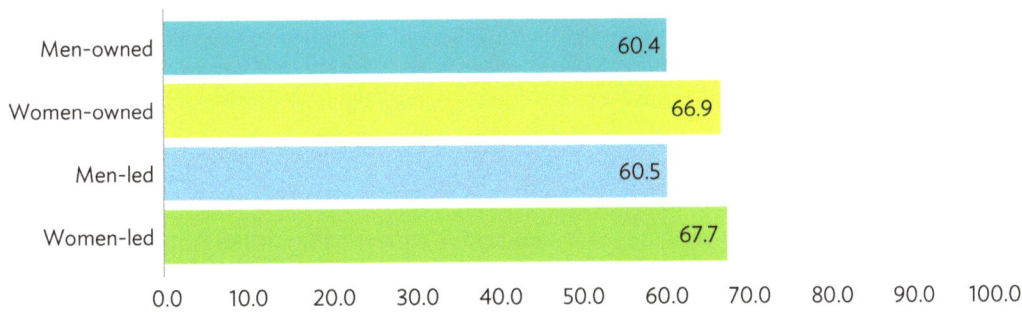

Men-owned	60.4
Women-owned	66.9
Men-led	60.5
Women-led	67.7

0.0   10.0   20.0   30.0   40.0   50.0   60.0   70.0   80.0   90.0   100.0

Source: Authors.

Figure 8: Cost of Business Registration for Ownership and Leadership by Gender

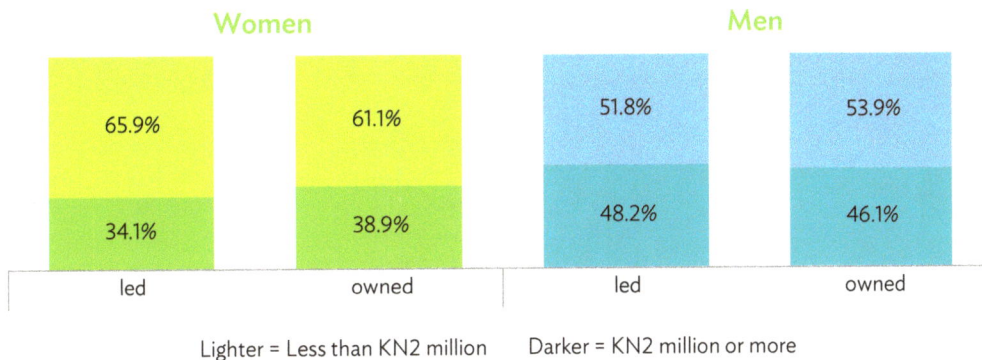

Women   Men

led	owned	led	owned
65.9%	61.1%	51.8%	53.9%
34.1%	38.9%	48.2%	46.1%

Lighter = Less than KN2 million   Darker = KN2 million or more

KN = kip.
Source: Authors.

Figure 8 shows that there is a variation in the cost of business registration by gender for leadership and ownership. Only one-third of women-owned and led enterprises reported they had to pay over KN2 million for business registration. Meanwhile, close to half of men-owned and led enterprises reported they had to pay over KN2 million for business registration. The survey shows that women-led enterprises paid on average KN2.1 million for business registration compared to KN2.7 million by men-led enterprises. Closer examination shows that this payment is relatively more costly for women-led enterprises. The median number of full-time workers in a women-led enterprise is six, whereas for the men-led enterprise it is 10, which means that relative to the size of the enterprise workforce, the payment of KN2.1 million is approximately one-third more costly to women-owned and women-led enterprises.[50]

The survey also found that women-led enterprises took less time to register their businesses than men-led enterprises. This is partly explained by the nature of the business activity undertaken and

[50]   The average payment for business registration by women-led companies was 79.3% (KN2.1 million/KN2.7 million) of that of men-led companies. The median size of a women-led company is 60% of the median size of men-led companies. The 32.0% is equal (79.3%–60%)/60%.

enterprise size. The construction and manufacturing businesses, where women's leadership and ownership is less common, incurred the longest delays in registration. For example, manufacturing businesses took an average of 31 days to complete registration. Part of the reason for this difference is the number of licenses that have to be obtained from different government departments at the same time as getting the enterprise registration certificate. Table 10 describes this difference showing that a retail store has to get a maximum of two licenses from two separate departments. In contrast a manufacturing business has to obtain up to 13 licenses, five of which are listed in the Table 10. This adds to the length of time taken and the cost of obtaining the licenses.

Table 10: Examples of Licenses Required for Different Business Activities

Sector	Number of Licenses	Examples of Licenses	Number of Women-Owned Enterprises[a]
Retail	2	• License to distribute agriculture tools, fertilizers, pesticides, seeds retail license (Agriculture and Forestry Department) • Business operating license for domestic trade business (wholesale and retail) (Department of Industry and Commerce)	56% of formalized women-owned enterprises operate in this sector compared to 15% of men-owned enterprises
Manufacturing of processed food business	13	• Factory operation certificate (Food and Drugs Department) • Permit to import packaged materials (Food and Drugs Department) • Import permit for food products (Food and Drugs Department) • Annual action plan for industrial processing factory (Department of Industry and Handicraft) • Certificate of prepackaged product inspection (Standardized and Measurement department)	3% of formalized women-owned enterprises operate in this sector compared to 10% of men-owned enterprises

[a] Ministry of Industry and Commerce. 2020. Lao People's Democratic Republic Gender Study 2020. p. 7.
Source: Inventory of Business Licenses http://www.bned.moic.gov.la/.

Micro and small enterprises were more likely than medium and large enterprises to complete registration in 10 days. However, average processing times were still prohibitive. Long and expensive registration processing is not an inducement to growing a formal private sector. Encouraging informal businesses to complete business registration and enter the formal economy requires improving the ease of registering a business.

3.   Transparency and Access to Information

Being able to find information easily, including the forms for registration and having access to an official one-stop website for information on complying with all regulations, is important for entrepreneurs deciding to enter the formal economy. Websites are an important avenue for accessing information that can be particularly useful for women with family commitments who are not able to leave home to attend a provincial registry office. It alleviates the need for rural dwellers to travel from their homes to registries in urban centers.

The 2017 ProFIT report issued a low score to all the provinces under this subindex. It urged provinces to improve the quality of websites, identifying this as an important factor for businesses. By 2019, 11 out of 17 provinces had an official website and the 2019 ProFIT report shows that three provinces had improved their score in this category: Savannakhet, Houaphan, and Phongsali. Gender-disaggregated data collected is not sufficient for identifying the impact on women at provincial level or for analyzing the manner in which these websites impacted on women-owned and women-led enterprises. Such data would be useful in future surveys.

Transparency and access to information were issues for all entrepreneurs. The ProFIT survey examined respondents' access to eight key documents,[51] with responses resulting in a continuing low score for both women and men (Figure 9). Women-led enterprises, in particular, reported lower performance on transparency with a score of 25.7 out of 100, compared to men-led enterprises with a score of 27.6 out of 100. Women-led enterprises gave lower scores compared to male-led enterprises across all enterprise size, with the exception of microenterprises (Figure 10).

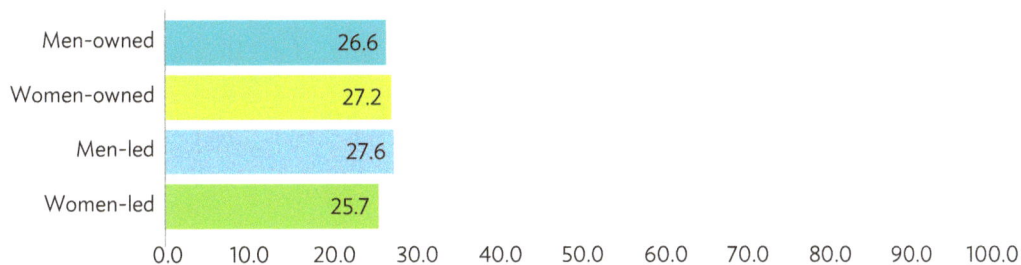

Figure 9: Transparency and Access to Information Subindex for Leadership and Ownership by Gender
(100-point scale)

Source: Authors.

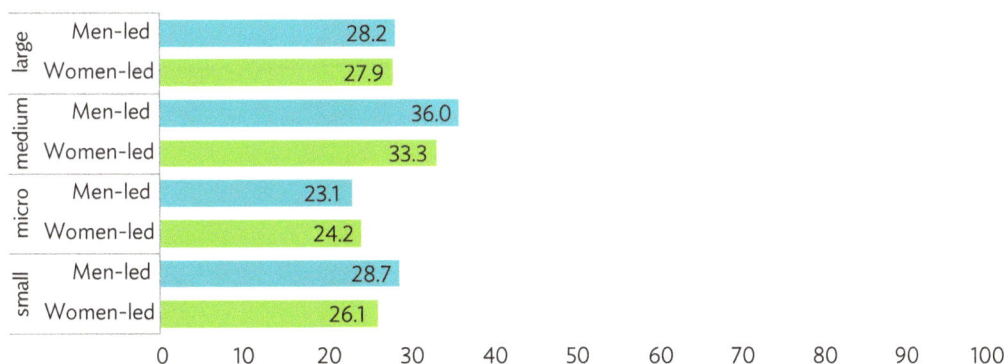

Figure 10: Transparency and Access to Information Subindex by Gender and Enterprise Size
(100-point scale)

Source: Authors.

---

[51] These documents are the provincial budget, socioeconomic development plan, regulations, instruction and agreement, investment budget for infrastructure development, land use strategic plan, investment promotion policy, procedures and forms, and public procurement opportunities.

Figure 11 looks at three key documents where the discrepancy between men-led and women-led enterprises was the greatest. The discrepancy between women-led and men-led enterprises on access to procedures and forms required for coordination with the government was 5.1%; access to provincial regulations, instruction, and agreement was 4.5%; and access to the provincial investment budget for infrastructure development was 4.0%. At first glance these differences may seem small. But when combined with the facts that there are fewer women-led enterprises operating in each of the geographical markets, and that women have less access to networks which are an important way of sharing information, it makes it much harder for women-led enterprises in comparison to those that are men-led, to operate effectively int he private sector. Further, women's poorer access to official documents may be linked to lower levels of literacy, lack of clarity in documents, and dissemination not being conducted in gender-sensitive manner.

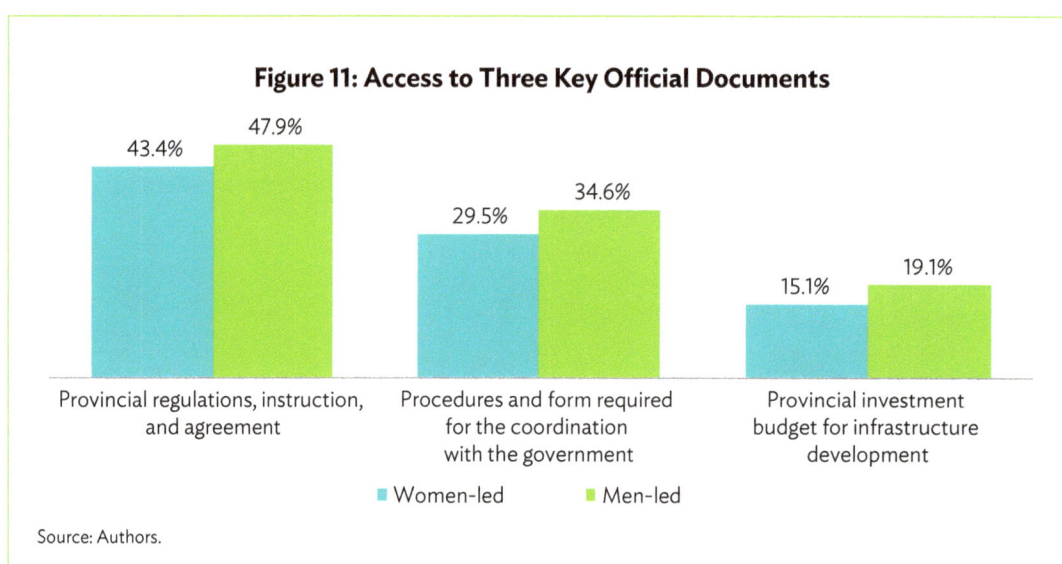

Figure 11: Access to Three Key Official Documents

Source: Authors.

4.   Regulatory Burden

This subindex is measured by three indicators: frequency of inspections by government agencies, time required to renew a TIN, and the cost of TIN renewal. Figure 12 shows that women-led enterprises reported lower costs and less time needed to renew their TINs. While 94.2% of women-led enterprises completed TIN renewal in less than a month, 91.7% of men-led enterprises did so in that time frame. Only 14.7% of women-led enterprises reported having to pay over KN3 million for renewing their TINs while this figure for men-led enterprises was 18.5%. This represents an improvement that is at least in part attributable to reforms initiated by PMO 02/2018.

At first glance, women-led enterprises appear to pay less for renewing TINs than their male counterparts. However, this payment is relatively more costly for women-led enterprises, which paid on average KN1.7 million for renewing TINs compared to KN2.1 million by men-led ones. The median number of full-time workers in a women-led enterprise is six, while for men-led enterprises it is at 10, which means in relative terms to the number of workers in the enterprise, the payment of KN1.7 million is one-third more costly for women-led enterprises.[52] The same logic can be applied when it comes to

---

[52]   The average payment for renewing TINs by women-led companies was 80% (KN1.7 million/KN2.1 million) of that of men-led companies. The median size of a women-led company is 60% of the median size of men-led companies. The 33% is equal (80%-60%)/60%.

the number of days required for processing TINs. Future efforts to have questions that distinguish all responses according to enterprise size will allow for improved analysis, along with a survey sample at a representative size that allows for disaggregation of data to complete further analysis.

Figure 12: Cost and Time for Renewing Tax Identification Number

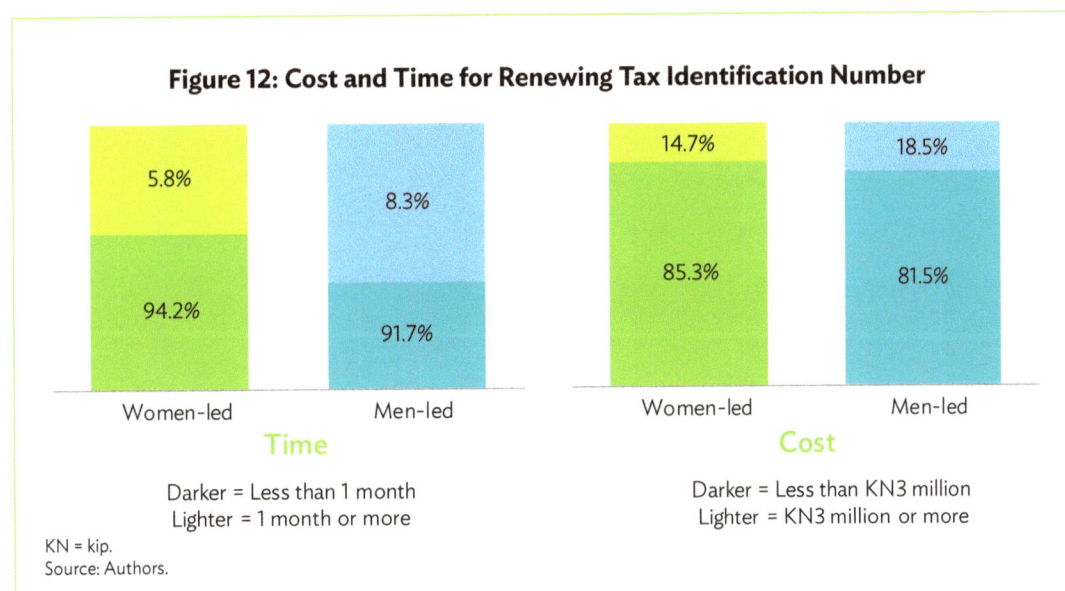

Time
- Darker = Less than 1 month
- Lighter = 1 month or more

Cost
- Darker = Less than KN3 million
- Lighter = KN3 million or more

KN = kip.
Source: Authors.

As discussed in chapter 2.C, only one in four women undertaking business activities had a registration certificate compared to one in three men. Future surveys could examine the regulatory burden on women working in different enterprise sizes. There is the likelihood that micro and small enterprises, where women dominate, find the costs and time involved to be more onerous than larger enterprises. As discussed in chapter 2.B, more women entrepreneurs choose to operate their business informally compared to men, citing inspections and meetings with government; and the time, fees and paperwork involved as deterrents. Recognition of the regulatory burden placed on micro and small enterprises may lead to designing specific policies that facilitate a transition from the informal to the formal economy.

5.   Informal Charges

Informal charges are not part of the fees paid to government departments, but are payments levied for accessing documents, renewing licenses and TINs, and negotiating official tax payments. Registration personnel and enterprise registrars are prohibited from soliciting such payments and applicants seeking registration are also prohibited from making such offerings.[53] Nevertheless, tax negotiations are common across all provinces, partly explained by the lack of bookkeeping systems in businesses, which necessitates inspections and discussions with inspectors on the taxable income of the enterprise.

---

[53] Government of the Lao PDR, Ministry of Industry and Commerce. Decision on Enterprise Registration January 2019, Articles 23 and 24. http://www.investlaos.gov.la/images/Announcement/MOIC_Decision_No.0023_on_Enterprise_Registration_Jan-9-2019-ENG-LAO.pdf.

Figure 13: Informal Charges Subindex for Leadership and Ownership by Gender
(100-point scale)

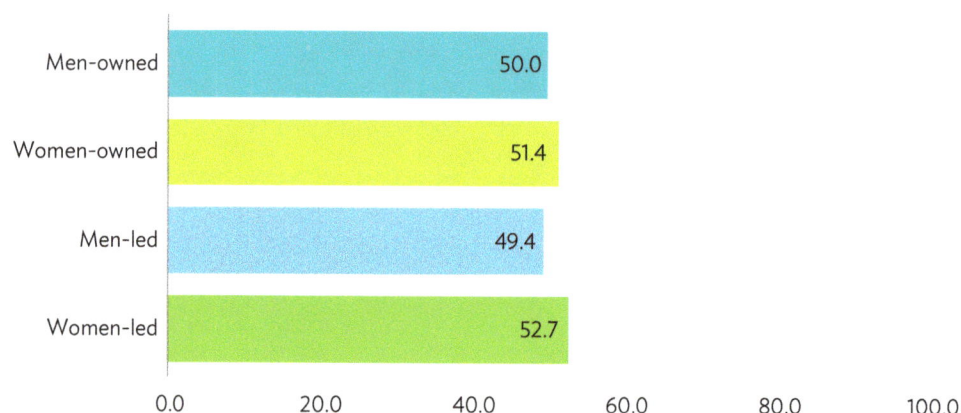

Source: Authors.

Figure 14: Selected Indicators of Informal Charges for Leadership and Ownership by Gender

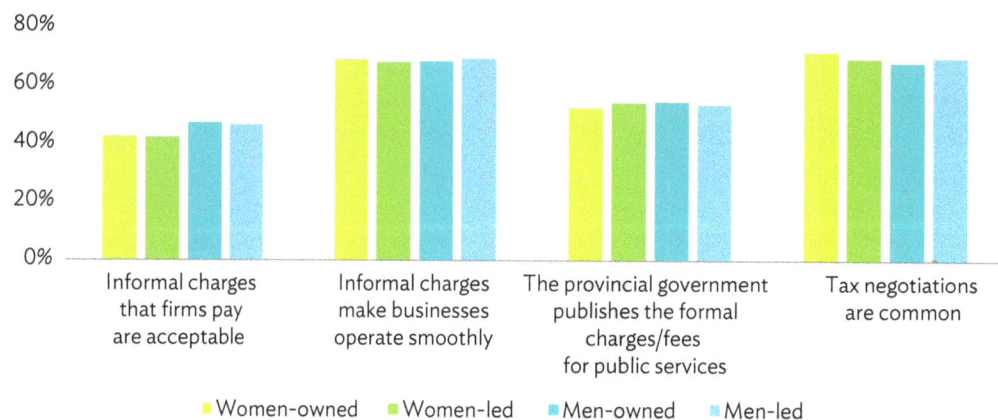

Source: Authors.

The 2019 ProFIT report found that approximately 70% of the 1,357 respondents who applied for a business registration, licenses, and permits paid informal charges.[54] Over 68% reported that informal payments were necessary to ensure efficient business operations, and 69% said that it was common to negotiate taxes. Figure 13 shows the informal charges subindex for enterprise leadership and ownership by gender. Women scored slightly higher than men, largely due to a lower relative share of informal charges to enterprise revenue. Women-owned enterprises scored 51.4 out of 100 on this subindex. However, when asked about informal charges, more women in leadership and ownership positions found them to be unacceptable (Figure 14).

---

[54]   ProFIT 2019 report, pp. 17–18.

Tax negotiations were extremely common for both women and men, and related to poor access to information and a perceived need to pay informal charges to ensure smooth business operations (Box). Two different tax reporting systems are available for business owners in the Lao PDR: (i) for enterprises with registered capital under KN1 billion, the enterprise is allowed to pay a lump-sum tax annually; and (ii) enterprises with registered capital of over KN1 million are required to declare their actual income and pay tax based on an accounting system.[55] Paying a lump sum involved more negotiations and informal charges. It has been reported that micro and small women-owned enterprises engage in cross-border trade, and driven by time constraints and home duties, are less likely to negotiate taxes proposed to them by authorities. This resulted in these women paying comparatively higher taxes entrepreneurs who negotiate their taxes, which has implications for business profitability and sustainability of these women. Women entrepreneurs stated that accounting programs were too expensive for their micro and small enterprises and few opted to use them.[56] However, accounting programs that keep up-to-date records of enterprise revenue offer the potential to mitigate against tax negotiations, by consolidating evidence of enterprise transactions and reducing discretionary estimates of revenue. Such benefits may offset costs of software and skills upgrading.

Box: Informal Practices in Business Operations in the Lao People's Democratic Republic

Informal practices in business operations include non-registration of operations, underreporting of enterprise income, payments to officials that are not part of the formal fees, and negotiations of taxes, among others. Firms also reported having to pay informal charges for accessing government documents as well as to authorities conducting business inspections. Among the respondents who submitted requests to the provincial governments for documents not publicly available, including provincial regulations, instructions, and agreements, 45% paid for informal charges to obtain the documents. Meanwhile, 35% of enterprises paid informal charges to government officials for inspections. The Provincial Facilitation for Investment and Trade (ProFIT) subindex on informal charges uses five indicators: informal charges as share of revenue; and four more indicators representing necessity, commonality, and acceptability of informal charges and public disclosure of formal charges (Table). Findings of the ProFIT survey indicate that informal practices in businesses operations are common and perceived to be part of routine operations, including payment of informal charges. More than two-thirds of the enterprises surveyed for this report disclosed that informal payments were necessary to run their operations.

Table: Informal Charges Subindex Indicators

Indicator	Weight (%)
Informal charges as a share of revenue	40
Acceptability of informal charges	15
Commonality of tax negotiations	15
Necessity of informal charges	15
Public disclosure of formal charges	15

Source: Authors.

---

[55] Footnote 34, p. 15.
[56] Footnote 34, p. 14.

6. Consistency in Policy Implementation

This subindex tracked business owners' responses to a series of questions including the consistency of implementation of national rules by provincial governments, their perceptions of the advantages of having personal connections, and their opinions on favoritism toward state-owned enterprises. Consistent application of rules is evidence of transparent decision-making and provides certainty to the business community, which is an essential prerequisite for creating trust in markets that in turn attracts entrepreneurs and investors. The need for national laws to be consistently applied is a demanding task that requires careful coordination and accountability. The 2017 ProFIT report stated the business community considered local governments were not good at implementing the central government's laws and regulations. In 2019, this skepticism about provincial governments' ability to implement the central government's rules continued. Figure 15 shows that women-led enterprises were more positive on policy implementation than men-led enterprises, while women's ownership of enterprises was linked to more negative views.

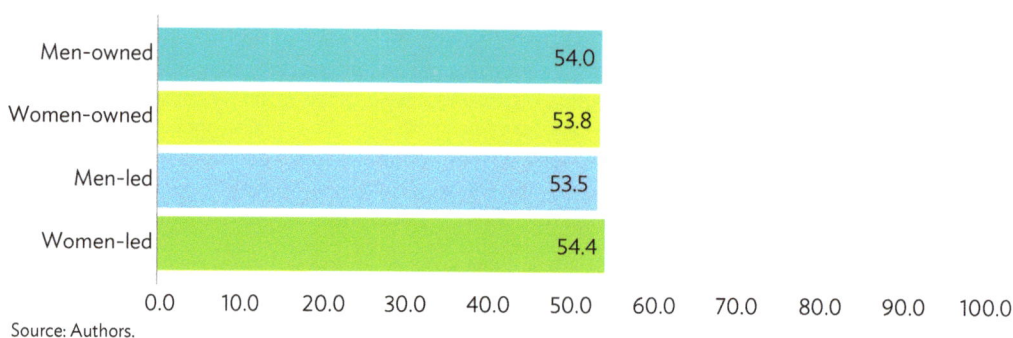

Figure 15: Consistency of Policy Implementation Subindex for Leadership and Ownership by Gender
(100-point scale)

Source: Authors.

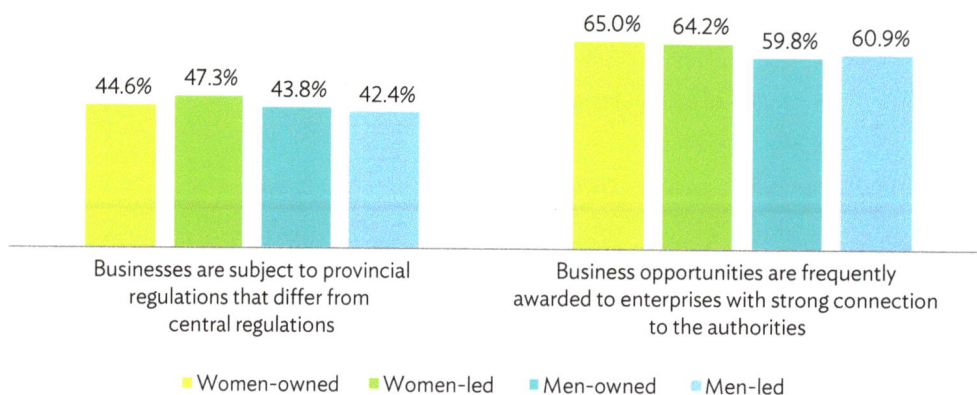

Figure 16: Selected Indicators of Consistency in Policy Implementation for Leadership and Ownership by Gender

Source: Authors.

Transparency in decision-making and policy implementation by central and provincial governments is important to build legitimacy and trust in the regulatory framework. Figure 16 deals with the respondents' perceptions of the advantages of having personal connections and consistency between policy at central and subnational levels. It shows the percentage of respondents that agreed with the statement that enterprises with connections to the local government received more contracts with the government, land, and other resources. Women-led and women-owned enterprises were more critical than men-led enterprises, with 64.2% and 65.0% in agreement, respectively. Women also had worse experiences in terms of businesses being subject to provincial regulations that differ from central regulations. Such a lack of trust in consistent and transparent decision-making is a significant barrier to attracting new businesses seeking to innovate and compete. As 92% of women-led enterprises are either micro or small enterprises, women-led and women-owned businesses lack this requisite trust.

7.   Business Friendliness

This subindex had four indicators including provincial government support for private local businesses and the application of new solutions to solve problems. Figure 17 presents the subindex results for enterprise leadership and ownership by gender, where perceived performance was better for women than men. It shows that both women and men in enterprises appreciated the support of their provincial governments, with women-led enterprises being more positive. Women-led enterprises scored 60.4 out of a total of 100 on this subindex, compared to men-led enterprises that scored 58.1.

This subindex also asked respondents about their awareness of PMO 02/2018. Figure 18 illustrates that there is a clear gap in knowledge of PMO 02/2018 for enterprise leadership and ownership when it comes to gender. While 24.4% of men-led enterprises were aware of this decree, only 17.7% of women-led enterprises reported awareness. As discussed in section 2.2, women's business networks, which is the main channel for building their awareness of new regulatory requirements, are not as developed as men's networks, and provides context for this result.

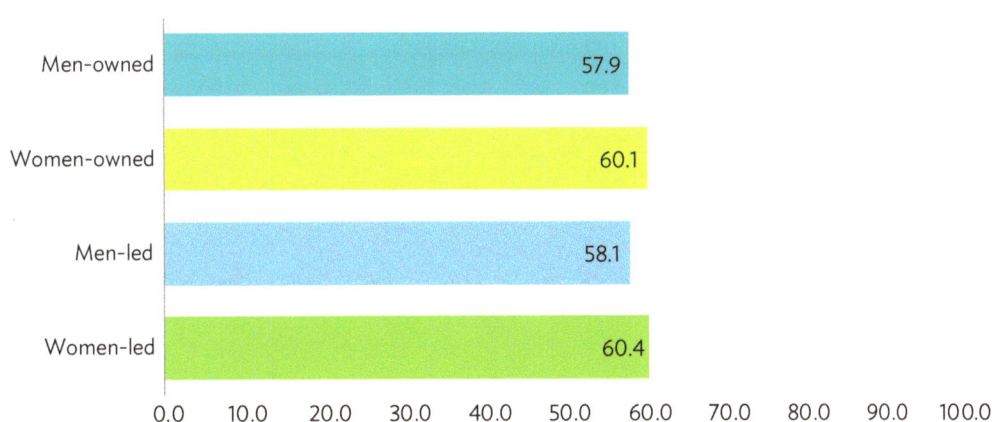

Figure 17: Business Friendliness Subindex for Leadership and Ownership by Gender
(100-point scale)

Source: Authors.

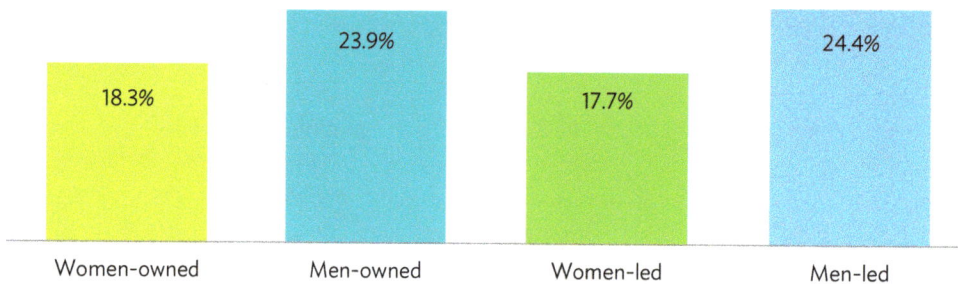

Figure 18: Knowledge of PMO 02/2018 for Leadership and Ownership by Gender

Women-owned	Men-owned	Women-led	Men-led
18.3%	23.9%	17.7%	24.4%

PMO = Prime Minister's Order.
Source: Authors.

Chapter 4

Selected Issues

A. Facilitating the Transition from the Informal to the Formal Economy

The 2020 Economic Census report confirms that 69.6% of enterprises operate informally, with more women's enterprises choosing to do so. Only one in four women had a registration certificate compared with one in three men, which indicates that the advantages of formalization are not perceived or are outweighed by the costs associated with complying with regulatory requirements for registration.

Incentivizing formalization will require a multipronged approach that makes the advantages of formalization clearer, reduces the costs associated with it, and smooths the way for those who seek to formalize with easy access to information and a simple one-stop online process.

The 2019 ProFIT survey reports on several costs imposed on the formalization of businesses, including the high cost of renewing the TIN and the necessity of paying informal charges. Micro and small businesses, with less business acumen, are more likely to confuse formal government taxes and fees, including the payment for registration, TINs, and official taxes with informal charges, which contributes to a lack of trust in government and a lack of transparency in decision-making.

This is reflected in the economic census where it is reported that only 12.9% of enterprises had a valid TIN, while 81.7% reported that they paid taxes through a daily tax ticket system rather than based on accounting declarations or contracted amounts. Women-led enterprises were less likely to secure a valid TIN than men-led enterprises, with only 10.9% of women-led enterprises holding such a document, compared with 15.5% of men-headed enterprises. This discrepancy may be indicative of several issues, including poor quality tax legislation and weak tax administration, low levels of knowledge on tax policy by authorities and taxpayers, lack of dissemination and awareness-raising on business regulations and tax policy, and absence of bookkeeping systems in enterprises. In general, the low prevalence of enterprises reporting that they hold TINs is an indicator that informal charges are being pursued and therefore are not good for private sector development or for public revenues.

Informal charges or "expediting fees" have historically been a part of the transaction costs associated with engaging in the formal economy. Studies have proposed that such payments can "grease the wheel" and ensure that businesses can overcome bureaucratic barriers and processes to succeed in the market.[57] Other empirical studies point to how such payments can "sand the wheels" of commerce, because corruption absorbs the returns from business activities and distorts entrepreneurial spirit and behavior, creates greater uncertainty among businesses that ultimately impacts their strategic or investment decisions, has an adverse impact on business innovation and growth, and places hurdles on foreign investment.[58]

Such charges weigh heavily on women- and men-owned and operated businesses at all levels in both the formal and informal economies. Businesses that operate in the informal economy are unlikely to come into contact with government officials, indicating that they therefore may have a chance of avoiding such payments, which acts as a disincentive to entering the formal economy.

It has been argued that not all enterprises are impacted in the same way by the pressure to make such payments. For example, in Viet Nam, it is the medium-sized enterprises based in Ha Noi, operating hotels, restaurants, and construction businesses, that suffer the most.[59] It was reported that

[57]   J. Rand and F. Tarp. 2012. Firm-level corruption in Vietnam. *Economic Development and Cultural Change* 60(3). pp. 571–595.

[58]   D. Maruichi and M. Abe. 2019. Corruption and the business environment in Vietnam: Implications from an empirical study. *Asia Pacific Policy Studies* 6. pp. 222–245.

[59]   Footnote 58, p. 240.

enterprises that are inspected are more likely to have to pay bribes than non-inspected enterprises (footnote 58). There is scope to collect further data at a provincial level on the impact that such charges have on women in enterprises in order to design suitable interventions. However, most importantly, it is essential that the costs and benefits of formalization outweigh those of remaining informal and micro and small entrepreneurs are made aware of these benefits.

B. Impact of PMO 02/2018 on Women in Enterprises

PMO 02/2018 intended to reduce the time and cost required for business registration. The 2019 ProFIT survey reports that the overall time required for processing registration decreased, in line with newly issued government regulations. Costs also decreased. Enterprises established in 2019 under new procedures paid on average KN1.7 million to register their business, while enterprises established under previous procedures spent an average of KN2.6 million. However, payments were still much higher than the officially required payments, indicating a persistence of payment of expediting fees by enterprises for meeting the government's regulatory requirements. The overall prevalence of providing informal payments to secure business licenses or for complying with government regulations also remained unchanged under new and old procedures.

Fewer women-led and women-owned enterprises reported that they had knowledge of PMO 02/2018. The responses by gender were significantly different and the lack of knowledge was evident across all enterprise sizes. This brings to the forefront that the current channels relied on to disseminate information about PMO 02/2018 is not reaching women entrepreneurs and highlights the importance of improving access to information, including women's awareness of business regulations that govern their livelihoods.

Knowledge of PMO 02/2018 had substantially different impacts on the time and cost associated with obtaining an enterprise registration certificate. Figure 19 illustrates that knowledge of PMO 02/2018 reduced the processing time more for men-led enterprises than women-led enterprises, while knowledge of PMO 02/2018 reduced the cost of registration more for women-led enterprises than men-led enterprises. However, with women having less knowledge of PMO 02/2018, the comparative gains in terms of time and cost for women-led enterprises was still less due to the gap in knowledge. Lower scores on transparency and access to information suggest that awareness-raising campaigns, including through public–private dialogues, have an important role to play in providing a more equitable business environment for both women and men business owners.

C. Collating Further Gender-Disaggregated Data for Assessment

The 2019 ProFIT survey assembled important gender-disaggregated data that enhance the understanding of women in enterprises. To develop a deeper understanding of how these enterprises function and design women-friendly policies, further gender-disaggregated data on the role of women in the private sector is needed. For example, questions on the actual involvement of the women in women-owned businesses would help to determine whether active or passive participation would be informative.

Further, gender-disaggregated data at the provincial level would add to the knowledge of subnational government efficacy for supporting an equitable business and investment climate.

Provincial-level data could also point out to the provinces that have encouraged more women entrepreneurs and could assist in identifying best practices for replication. Distinguishing all the responses from the sample according to enterprise size will allow for improved analysis of the needs of different types of entrepreneurs.

Additionally, focus group interviews that provide qualitative data should be considered in future surveys. Such data would add to the gender analysis.

Figure 19: Time and Cost to Obtain an Enterprise Registration Certificate with Knowledge of PMO 02/2018 by Gender

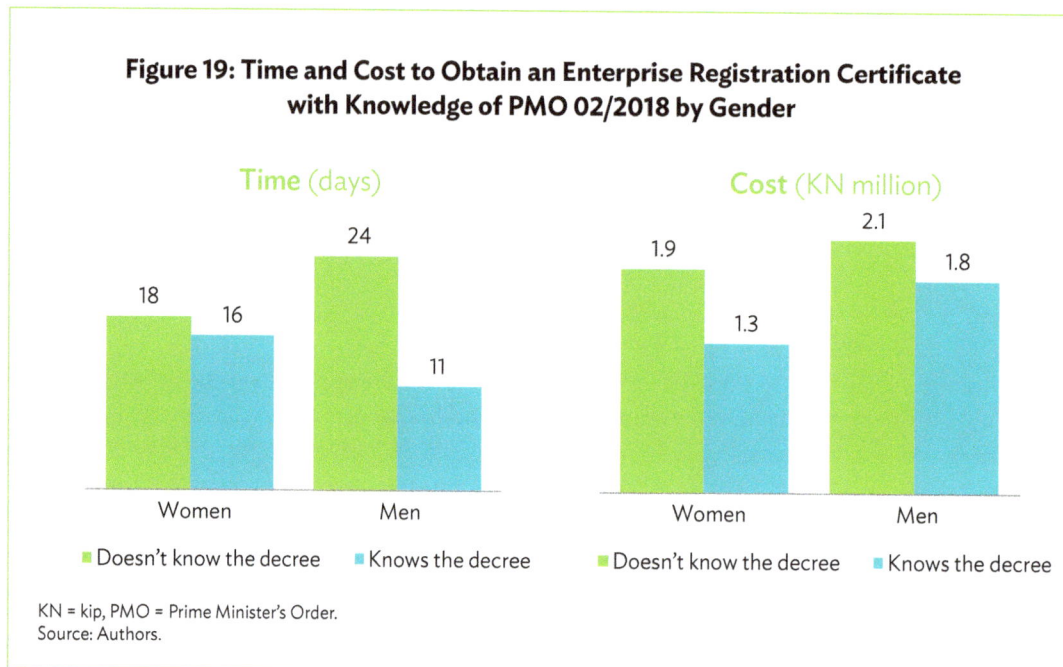

Time (days)

- Women: Doesn't know the decree 18, Knows the decree 16
- Men: Doesn't know the decree 24, Knows the decree 11

Cost (KN million)

- Women: Doesn't know the decree 1.9, Knows the decree 1.3
- Men: Doesn't know the decree 2.1, Knows the decree 1.8

■ Doesn't know the decree   ■ Knows the decree

KN = kip, PMO = Prime Minister's Order.
Source: Authors.

Chapter 5

Conclusions and Policy Implications

This report finds an improvement in business environment governance, with PMO 02/2018 driving a reduction in the cost and time of registering businesses in enterprises across provinces. The collection of gender-disaggregated data in the ProFIT survey makes it possible to assess how both women and men conduct business in the Lao PDR, which is a significant step toward inclusive business environment governance.

The Lao PDR's gender equality laws are aimed at meeting international obligations, but do not yet address equity issues in the private sector. Women's business activities are shaped by sociocultural norms, which makes it easier for women to participate in microenterprises from home, while managing care-giving responsibilities with limited capital, usually obtained through savings or from family members. These norms impact on how women participate in businesses, access markets, and build networks in multiple ways.

Women have long been operating businesses both in the informal and formal economies. More women operate their businesses informally without a registration certificate or a business permit. Their reluctance to formalization is partially explained by a perceived higher regulatory burden in relation to enterprise size and enterprise business activities. The majority of women-owned enterprises are micro or small. Women also choose to operate in trade, services, and small-scale manufacturing, where business registration and formalization is less common.

The experience of women and men in the world of work is not the same. There is a deficit of knowledge concerning government policies for the business environment among the private sector. The findings of this study indicate that women have less access to official documents, pay more for business registration, and for renewing their TIN in comparison to men-owned and -led enterprises. This knowledge deficit results in women-owned and women-led enterprises bearing a comparatively greater cost burden when running their business.

The analysis presented in this report points to several areas of improvement including providing for online business registration, building informative provincial government websites, and developing online platforms for government services. The following actions provide concrete recommendations to improve equity in the business environment in areas that target regulatory compliance, usage of tools to enable enterprise growth, and more agile policy responses.

1. Improve regulatory compliance by consolidating requirements.

(i) Adopt e-business registration.

Electronic business or e-business registration were adopted in Viet Nam and Myanmar, and is both time- and cost- effective. Women can benefit significantly from such a process as it alleviates the need for travel to provincial offices and enables them to complete the registration process outside office hours. It can also mitigate against informal charges and increase transparency. However, given that the majority of women-led enterprises are micro and small enterprises, the need for providing access to and familiarity with operating online systems and providing for transferring funds electronically will require consideration. Training programs in the use of information technology tools, run through the Lao PDR's civil society organizations in conjunction with government, will be important in implementing electronic business registration procedures.

(ii) **Improve awareness of business registration portal and inventory of business licenses.**
An updated portal that provides information in one location of all licenses, permits, certificates, and authorizations has been established by Ministry of Industry and Commerce. It is an important tool to improve transparency and confidence in the government. Increasing awareness of this portal by providing links through chambers of commerce, civil society organizations, and women's organizations will improve inclusive access.

(iii) **Implement a one-stop system.**
The recommendation made in PMO 02/2018 to implement a one-stop mechanism should be revisited and informed by the experience in other countries. It has the potential to create a more transparent and accessible registration system. Myanmar's experience suggests that such an online system should be supplemented by having computers and professionals who are able to assist people seeking to register their business. As many women have reported that they have limited ICT skills, incorporating appropriate help desks will be of assistance for women entrepreneurs. These services should be delivered at the provincial levels.

(iv) **Develop a coherent rationale for the licensing regime.**
While the adoption of a risk-based approach to licensing has been championed by the Ministry of Industry and Commerce, it has not been incorporated into practice. Doing so would result in a business only have to obtain a business license where the risks the business may generate such as risks to the health and safety of consumers or to the environment are significant. Implementing such an approach could result in certain low-risk micro businesses, such as trade stores or guesthouses, where women entrepreneurs dominate, being exempt from obtaining licenses.

(v) **Reform licensing and inspection.**
The current practice of requiring businesses to obtain licenses prior to commencing operations (ex ante) does not align with international licensing practice that favors monitoring and inspection once the operations have commenced (ex post). In effect, the business is allowed to start and is monitored through inspections when its operations are underway in order to assess high-risk activities. The main challenge to adopting such an approach is the widespread role of informal charges with 35% of enterprises reporting that they had paid such charges to inspection officials. Adopting an ex-post approach would have to be accompanied by greater controls on the discretionary powers of inspectors.

(vi) **Further integrate social security enrollment in business registration processes.**
Limited development of the social protection framework within the country, including integration of social security systems with the business regulatory environment, weakens private sector resilience to shocks. In the absence of reforms to address these issues, persistence of inequality of outcomes and opportunities will continue. Integrating registration to social security will require cooperation between government departments contributing to inclusive development.

(vii) **Enforce regulations prohibiting informal charges.**
Although there are clear rules prohibiting public officials and registration personnel from taking informal payments from enterprises, it is still common practice. Remedies to the situation remain ineffective and have not changed public perception or organizational practice. Solving issues that hinder the application of the rule of law will demonstrate government's efforts to improve the regulatory environment.

2.   Optimize utilization of growth enablers.

(i)   **Increase awareness of the benefits of formalization.**
Available data indicates that nearly 70% of entrepreneurs operate informally, supporting the conclusion that the benefits of formalization are not understood. Provincial governments in collaboration with the Lao Women's Union and financial institutions could develop a hub conducting a series of activities that link ICT training and awareness of financial products. There is potential for other civil society organizations to partner in such initiatives.

(ii)   **Improve access to finance.**
The lack of access to commercial finance has been identified as an important obstacle to starting or growing a business. Partnering with financial institutions to adopt alternative credit ratings systems, digital platforms, and designing financial products for women entrepreneurs is needed to address these obstacles.

(iii)   **Support targeted interventions for promoting ICT usage.**
Women have not had as much experience with ICT, with the 2020 Economic Census finding that 94.6% of women-led enterprises did not have any familiarity with using ICT. Interventions to promote ICT usage include: (i) raising awareness of benefits for productivity and competitiveness, (ii) promoting development of virtual marketplaces through digital platform providers, (iii) supporting digital market making and business-matching enterprise fairs, (iv) providing a range of self-paced individual training modules at one-stop shops, and (v) promoting design sprint training workshops for businesswomen to enhance problem-solving through leveraging ICT solutions.

(iv)   **Design policies for micro and small enterprises.**
Micro and small enterprises have different needs from larger enterprises. Designing targeted policies that address their needs, rather than adopting a generic policy, should be considered. For example, many businesswomen report difficulties in accessing markets, and online markets in particular. Creating online marketplaces at a provincial level has the potential to assist women with such access.

(v)   **Strengthen women's business platforms.**
Women's business platforms can provide their members with business development services. While they so far have provided broad based training and savings programs have been implemented, targeted training to assist women develop marketing skills, access online distribution channels, integrate accounting processes and tender for public procurement contracts will assist in developing successful and sustained private sector participation.

3.   Enable agile policy responses from government.

(i)   **Collate and make available further gender-disaggregated data at a provincial level.**
Plans to collate gender-disaggregated data, circumvented during COVID-19, should recommence for future ProFIT surveys. Further consideration may be given to collate information on the following areas: (a) all data should be distinguished on the basis of the size of the enterprise, (b) questions on decision-making within family businesses to better understand the situation of women that have their own enterprises should be included, (c) informal charges paid by women-

led enterprises at a provincial level should be interrogated, and (d) gender-disaggregated data at a provincial level should be obtained. Such data should be made publicly available to civil society and partners assisting in formulating inclusive private sector development.

(ii) **Collaborate with global corporations and government to introduce women-friendly procurement policies.**
The study confirms that half of all women-led enterprises recognized that access to business networks was an important aspect of successfully bidding for public and private contracts. Legislating for quotas requiring such contracts to benefit both women-led and men-led enterprises would provide better opportunities for women entrepreneurs.

(iii) **Manage talent and develop human capital for better governance.**
The capacity of government officials to improve the regulatory environment for businesses can be enhanced by investing in capacity to improve information systems and data management. Online capacity-building and training methods and systems need to be upgraded, with investments needed in curriculum. Digital literacy has become an important competence, along with skills in strategy and decision-making. Investment in these areas would contribute to improvements in governance and a strengthening of effectiveness of decision-making needed for improving the business environment.

(iv) **Provide training on hidden gender bias and gender mainstreaming for inclusive governance.**
Institutional bias has been identified as an important constraint that counters the implementation of gender equality laws and regulations. Training workshops on gendered outcomes and hidden bias can assist in addressing shifting institutional practice. Further, the employment of women officers to assist with inquiries from women entrepreneurs has proven successful in other jurisdictions and could be considered.

Appendix 1

Key Interviewees

Interviews were undertaken with six representatives from six different organizations. The purpose of the interviews was to identify any differences that the interviewees saw between men-led and women-led businesses.

The interviews were semi-structured, using the same eight questions. Male entrepreneurs were interviewed to provide their perspectives on the same questions to enable the team to assess if there were any different views between male and female entrepreneurs.

The persons interviewed and the organizations they belonged to are:

(i)   Valy Vetsaphone, vice-president of Lao National Chamber of Commerce and Industry (LNCCI), general manager of Kanyamitaphap, and IX National Parliament member
(ii) Souphaphone Sounnavong, general manager of Toh Lao group, LNCCI Board, and deputy director of the Lao Women's Entrepreneurial Association
(iii) Oulathai, general manager of Kristaphong Group, and Land Mark Hotel, and vice-president of Lao Young Entrepreneur
(iv) Ninpaseuth Xaingaphongsy, director of Women's Development Department, Lao Women's Union
(v)   Xaibandit Latsaphonh, vice-president of LNCCI, director of Lao Garment and Textile Association
(vi) Phongsavanh Phomkong, Head of office, International Finance Corporation

Eight questions were used in the interviews. The first seven were asked of all participants and the last one was only directed to women participants. The questions were:

(i)   What do you think are the main challenges for a female to start and conduct her business? What factors are effective for any challenges that may happen?
(ii)   Do male counterparts face the same or different challenges? What about the severity of these challenges? Are they more difficult for females or males, and why?
(iii) Do you find any differences in business regulations between female and male businesses?
(iv)   What do you think of the enforcement of rules on women-led businesses and male ones? Are they subject to the same or different enforcement? Do you find any advantage or disadvantages against women-led businesses in the enforcement of rules and laws?
(v)   Do you think the government or society provide an opportunity to females to be a business leader similar to males? What is your husband/family member's view?
(vi)   What do you think of the roles of women-led businesses in their contribution to the economy (important, not important, or normal)?
(vii) Which policy or measure should be adopted to promote women-led businesses?
(viii) What inspired you to be a businesswoman?

ProFIT Questionnaire 2019

Provincial Facilitation for Investment and Trade Index (ProFIT Index 2019)

Lao National Chamber of Commerce and Industry (LNCCI) thanks you for joining us in this survey. The survey gives you a unique opportunity to rate the local business environment and improve the business environment for your company. The LNCCI warrants that all information gathered shall be kept in strict confidence and your business will not be impacted.

1. Your name: _____   2. Position: _____

3. Mobile phone: _____   4. Email: _____

5. Your company business registration No: _____

6. Have you ever participated in assessment on provincial facilitation for investment and trade organized by LNCCI in 2017?

1 ☐ Yes   0 ☐ No

A. General information about your enterprise

A1. Company name and address: _____

A2. When is your company is established? _____

A3. Your province *

code	province	code	province
1	Phongsali	9	Vientiane
2	Louangnamtha	10	Vientiane Capital
3	Oudomxai	11	Bolikhamxai
4	Bokeo	12	Khammouan
5	Louangphabang	13	Savannakhet
6	Houaphan	14	Salavan
7	Xaignabouli	15	Xekong
8	Xiangkhouang	16	Champasak
		17	Attapu

A4. Gender of your managing director

0 ☐ Female   1 ☐ Male

A5. Do woman shareholders/owners have equal or more than 30% ownership

1 ☐ Yes   0 ☐ No

A6. Which sector does your company operate in?

1 ☐ Production   2 ☐ Services   3 ☐ Manufacturing

4 ☐ Construction   5 ☐ Agriculture, forestry, fisheries

6 ☐ Trading, whole, sales and retailing

7 ☐ Other:

A7. What are your main products/services? _____

A8. Type of company

1 ☐ Ordinary partnership   2 ☐ Limited liability partnership

3 ☐ Public company   4 ☐ Limited company

A9. Number of full-time workers? _____ people

A10. Did you expand your business in 2018?

1 ☐ Yes   0 ☐ No

A11. Do you plan to expand your business in 2019 and 2020?

1 ☐ Yes   0 ☐ No

B. Starting a business

B1. How did you obtain your business registration, operating license and permits to start your business?

1 ☐ Filed by myself or by my staff

0 ☐ Use external services (law, consulting firm, consultant)

B2. How did your company receive business license?

1 ☐ Receive business license the same time with tax identification number

2 ☐ Receive business license did not the same time with tax identification number

3 ☐ Other (specify) _____

B2.1 How many days did it take to complete your company registration (i.e., from submission of all the documents until receipt of company seal and registration certificate)
Total time spent (official working day) _____ days

B2.2 How much did you spend on obtaining business registration including all formal and informal charges (in Million LAK) _____

B.2.3. Do you think companies in your sector will have to pay informal charges to obtain the business registration?

1 ☐ Yes   0 ☐ No.

B3. Did you have to obtain an operating license and other permits to start your business

1 ☐ Yes (answer 3.1.1-3.3.5)   0 ☐ No (answer B4)

B3.1 Please let us know the name of the operating license and permit and the agencies that issues them, day took for obtain the license, and cost to obtain the license and permit?

No. 1	Name of licensee	Time (days)	Cost (Million KIP)
B.3.1.1			
B3.1.2			
B3.1.3			

B3.2 Do you think companies in your sector will have to pay informal charges to obtain the following licenses and permits?

1 ☐ Yes (answer B3.2.1)   0 ☐ No (answer B4)

B3.2.1 If yes, please specify the name of the licenses and permits

No. 1 _____

No. 2 _____

No. 3 _____

B4. Please tell us your experience in completing the following procedures for business registration.

Business establishment	The most difficult	Least difficulty	Not difficulty at all	Don't know
B4.1 Business license	3	2	1	9
B4.2 Tax certificate	3	2	1	9
B4.3 Company seal	3	2	1	9
B4.4 Operating license	3	2	1	9
B4.5 Amending business license	3	2	1	9
B4.6 Others (specify) _____	3	2	1	9

C. Transparency And Access To Information

C1. Please let us know whether the below documents are published by the local government or accessible by anybody

Document	Yes	No	Don't know
C11 Provincial budget	1 ☐	2 ☐	9 ☐
C12 Provincial Socio-economic development plan	1 ☐	2 ☐	9 ☐
C13 Provincial regulations, instruction, and agreement	1 ☐	2 ☐	9 ☐
C14 Provincial investment budget for Infrastructure development	1 ☐	2 ☐	9 ☐
C15 Provincial Land-Use strategic plan	1 ☐	2 ☐	9 ☐
C16 Provincial investment promotion policy	1 ☐	2 ☐	9 ☐
C17 Procedures and Form required for the coordination with the Government	1 ☐	2 ☐	9 ☐
C18 Public procurement opportunities	1 ☐	2 ☐	9 ☐

C2. Have you ever submitted a request for information or documents that are not publicly available, from the provincial government?

1 ☐ Yes (answer C2.1-C2.2)   0 ☐ No (answer C3)

C2.1. Did you receive all the information as requested?

1 ☐ Yes, I received all the information

2 ☐ No, I did not receive any information

3 ☐ I only received part of information requested

C2.2. Do you think companies like yours will he to pay any informal charge to the government officers to get those documents?

1 ☐ Yes   0 ☐ No

C3. Did you have a chance to provide comments on the draft policy or regulations of the province?

1 ☐ Yes   0 ☐ No

D. Regulatory Burden

D1. How many times was your business inspected by the provincial authorities in 2018?

_____

D2. Compared to 2017, what was the frequency of inspection by the provincial government?

3 ☐ More often   2 ☐ Less often   1 ☐ No difference

D3. Which of the following agencies inspected and examined your firm in 2018?

Document	Yes	No
Tax authority	1	0
Police authority	1	0
Industry and Commerce Authority	1	0
Line agency that issues operating license	1	0
Environment protection authority	1	0
Labor and social wealth-fare authority	1	0
Other, please specify _____	1	0

D4. Do you think the inspection of these authorities overlap or duplicate?

1 ☐ Yes   0 ☐ No

D5. Do you think companies like yours will have to pay informal charges to the inspector for each inspection by the government?

1 ☐ Yes   2 ☐ No

D6. How many days did it take you to renew your tax ID?
Total time spent (official working days) _____ days

D7. Please let us know how much did it cost you to renew your tax ID (TIN) in million LAK?
Total formal payment _____ Million Kip

D8. How many days did it take you to renew your operating license in 2018?
Total time spent (official working days) _____ days

D9. How much did it cost you to renew your operating license in 2018 (in Million LAK)?
Total formal payment _____ Million Kip

E. Informal Charges

E1. On average, what percentages of YOUR REVENUE do firms like yours typically pay per year for informal charges to public officials?

_____

E2. Do you believe that the amount of informal charges that firms like yours pay when engaging with government are acceptable?

1 ☐ Yes   0 ☐ No

E3. Do you think that it is common for the firms to pay extra "informal charges" to ensure that the business operation can be executed smoothly and easily?

1 ☐ Yes   0 ☐ No

E4. Does the provincial government publish the informal charges/fees for their services to the public?
1 ☐ Yes   9 ☐ No

E5. Do you believe that it is common to negotiate your taxes in your business sector?
1 ☐ Yes   9 ☐ No

F. Consistency in Policy Implementation

F1. Do you believe that the province implements central policy and regulation consistently?
1 ☐ Yes   0 ☐ No

F2. Do you believe that the different departments in the province work together well to support businesses?
1 ☐ Yes   0 ☐ No

F3. Are you subject to additional provincial regulations on business that differ from central regulations?
1 ☐ Yes (Answer F3.1)   0 ☐ No (answer F4)

F3.1 if yes, what is the impact of the additional provincial business regulations on your businesses?
1 ☐ Positive   2 ☐ Negative   3 ☐ The same

F4. Do you think the provincial government support the local private sector more than state-owned companies?
1 ☐ Yes   0 ☐ No   2 ☐ the same treatment

F5. Do you think the provincial government procurement contracts, land and other business resources mostly fall into the hands of enterprises that have strong connection with the provincial authorities?
1 ☐ Yes   0 ☐ No

G. Business Friendliness of the Provincial Government

G1. Do you think the provincial government have positive attitude toward the private sector?
1 ☐ Yes   2 ☐ No

G2. Is the provincial government helpful to the private sector?
1 ☐ Yes   0 ☐ No

G3. Do you think the provincial government is willing to improve and apply new solutions to solve problems and constraints that the private sector is facing?

1 ☐ Yes   0 ☐ No

G4. Do you know about the Prime Minister Decree No 02 on improvement regulation and coordinating mechanism on doing business in the Lao PDR?

1 ☐ Yes (answer G5)   0 ☐ No (answer G7)

G5. Do you think Decree 02/PM would help improve the business environment in your province?

1 ☐ Yes (answer G5.1)   2 ☐ No (answer G5.2)   3 ☐ Do not know (answer G7)

G5.1 If yes, how does it improve business environment?

Business environment	Yes	No
1. Procedure of business establishment is more convenient and clearer (easier to start a company)	1	0
2. Cost of business establishment decreased (lower cost of business registration)	1	0
3. Entrepreneurs can access to business information (better access to business information)	1	0
4. Government operation is more transparency (Greater transparency)	1	0
5. Procedure of issuing operating license is faster and the fee is reasonable (faster issuance of operating licenses)	1	0
6. Others (specify) _____	1	0

G5.2 If your answer no, why does it do not improve business environment?

Business environment	Yes	No
1. Procedure of business establishment does not much improvement	1	0
2. Cost of business establishment remained high	1	0
3. Entrepreneurs cannot access to business information	1	0
4. Government operation is less transparency	1	0
5. Procedure of issuing operating license is still complicated and high costs	1	0
6. Others (specify)_____	1	0

G6. Which of the following actions would strengthen implementation of Decree 02?

1 ☐ Apply e-government to business registration (Multiple choice)

2 ☐ Apply e-tax filing and payment

3 ☐ Improve coordination between government agencies

4 ☐ Concrete timetable for reducing and simplifying business regulations and licenses

5 ☐ Other: _____

G7. In the last year, did your firm use the following services in the province? If yes, please specify the providers? Services	No, don't use the service	Yes, from which service provider		
		Provided by provincial agencies	Provided by private sectors in the province	Provided by the Private Organizations (Chamber of Commerce and Business Association)
	(1)	(2)	(3)	(4)
G71. Market information research	0	1	2	3
G72. Legal consultancy	0	1	2	3
G73. Recruitment	0	1	2	3
G74. Business matchmaking	0	1	2	3
G75. Trade promotion and trade fair / exhibition services	0	1	2	3
G76. Technology-related training program	0	1	2	3
G77. Training on Accounting and Finance	0	1	2	3
G78. Training on Business Administration	0	1	2	3
G79. Capacity building for the private sectors	0	1	2	3
10. Others (Please identify _____)	0	1	2	3

G8. Please rank the priority of the sections listed above– what should be prioritized by the provincial government to support the private sectors in the province? (1 means the highest priority and 5 means the lowest priority)

	1, highest priority	2	3	4	5, lowest priority
Make it easier to start a business	1	2	3	4	5
Improve transparency and access to information	1	2	3	4	5
Reduce regulatory burden	1	2	3	4	5
Improve consistency in policy implementation	1	2	3	4	5
Be more friendly to private sector	1	2	3	4	5

G8. Additional comments on improving business environment in your province?

References

Asian Development Bank and World Bank. 2012. *Country Gender Assessment for Lao PDR. Reducing Vulnerability and Increasing Opportunity*. Manila and Washington, DC.

Government of the Lao People's Democratic Republic (Lao PDR). 2013. *President's Decree No. 170/PD. Dated 20 August, 2013 on Promulgation of Lao Women Union Law*. Vientiane: National Assembly, Government of the Lao PDR.

_____. 2015. *President's Decree No. 031/PD. Dated 30 January, 2015 on Promulgation of Combating and Preventing Violence Against Women Law*. Vientiane: National Assembly, Government of the Lao PDR.

_____. 2020. *President's Decree No. 029/PD. Dated 09 January, 2020 on Promulgation of the Law of Gender Equality*. Vientiane: National Assembly, Government of the Lao PDR.

_____. 2004. *President's Decree No. 70/Lao PDR on Promulgation of Development and Women Protection*. 15 November. Vientiane: National Assembly, Government of the Lao PDR.

Government of the Lao PDR, Ministry of Industry and Commerce. 2020. *Lao PDR Gender Study, 2020*. Vientiane.

Government of the Lao PDR, Ministry of Planning and Investment. 2016. The 8th Five-Year National Socio-Economic Development Plan (2015–2020). Vientiane.

International Finance Corporation (IFC). 2018. *IFC Banking on Women: Business Case Update No. 2, Lower NPLs for Women-Led SMEs*. Washington, DC.

Keovialey, R. 2018. *Overview of Women's Entrepreneurship in Micro, Small and Medium Enterprises in Lao PDR*.

Lao Business Women's Association. 2018. *Lao Business Women's Survey in 2018*.

Lao National Chamber of Industry and Commerce. 2018 and 2020. *Provincial Facilitation for Investment and Trade Index (ProFIT). Measuring Economic Governance of Commerce and Industry*.

Lao Statistics Bureau. 2020. Economic Census III. Vientiane.

Malesky, E., P. T. Ngoc, and P. N. Thach. 2021. *The Vietnam Provincial Competitiveness Index: Measuring Economic Governance for Private Sector Development, 2020 Final Report*. Ha Noi: Vietnam Chamber of Commerce and Industry and United States Agency for International Development.

A Case Study of Lao PDR. Vientiane: Ministry of Industry and Commerce. pp. 1–30.

United Nations Children's Fund (UNICEF). 2021. *Impact of COVID-19 on Reimagining Gender*. Vientiane. https://lao.unfpa.org/sites/default/files/pub-pdf/covid-19_impact_assessment_lao_pdr-_brief_gender.pdf.

United Nations Development Programme (UNDP). 2015. *Sustainable Development Goals: Gender Equality*. Vientiane: UNDP.

_____. 2017. *Gender Equality in Lao PDR, Sustainable Development Goals*. Vientiane Capital: UNDP.

_____. 2018. *Sustainable Development Goals: Gender Equality: Why It Matters*. New York: UNDP.

World Bank. 2018. *The World Bank Enterprise Surveys 2017 for manufacturing and service sectors*. Washington, DC: The World Bank Group.

_____. 2019. *Lao PDR Economic Monitor, Maintaining Economic Stability. Constraints to doing business for SMES*. Vientiane: The World Bank Group.

_____. 2021. *Women, Business and the Law Report 2021*. Washington, DC: The World Bank Group.

World Economic Forum. 2021. *Global Gender Gap Report 2021*. Geneva: WEF.